MY WARS AND IN BETWEEN

A Memoir

LT. COL. JAMES S. OLIVER, USAF (RET.)
LOUISE K. OLIVER

MY WARS AND IN BETWEEN
A MEMOIR

iUniverse books may be ordered through booksellers or by contacting:

iUniverse
1663 Liberty Drive
Bloomington, IN 47403
www.iuniverse.com
1-800-Authors (1-800-288-4677)

Because of the dynamic nature of the Internet, any web addresses or links contained in this book may have changed since publication and may no longer be valid. The views expressed in this work are solely those of the author and do not necessarily reflect the views of the publisher, and the publisher hereby disclaims any responsibility for them.

Any people depicted in stock imagery provided by Thinkstock are models, and such images are being used for illustrative purposes only. Certain stock imagery © Thinkstock.

ISBN: 978-1-4917-8685-7 (sc)
ISBN: 978-1-4917-8687-1 (hc)
ISBN: 978-1-4917-8686-4 (e)

Library of Congress Control Number: 2015921491

Print information available on the last page.

iUniverse rev. date: 02/17/2016

To Reece "Gus" Augustus and Flora Carbonell Oliver, Papa and
Mama—my resourceful, brave, dedicated, proud parents;

Louise Kuhn Oliver, my assistive, helpful, and supportive
wife, who comforted me when PTSD episodes significantly
affected me several times during this project;

Fé Rebecca Oliver, my little sis, Becky, who just days before
she died of cancer admonished that I must soon publish my
recollections lest they become lost to the world forever;

Eddie and Manolo, two very brave twelve-year-olds who lost
their lives while ensuring my family's survival; and

the United States of America, my beautiful country and my home.

Contents

Preface

I titled this memoir *My Wars and In Between: A Memoir* because it is a collection of memories spanning my lifetime. It covers my recollections from my childhood development years to the present. A little sleight of hand is played when I write about my three wars. Since this is a collection of memories of wars in which I have personally participated, it treats WWII, the Cold War, and the Vietnam War as if they occurred serially. In other words, one war follows the next, just as historians like to treat wars— all neatly tied together as a package. That is how my wars are featured. It so happens that my military career—all twenty-four years of active duty in the US Air Force—played out exactly that way.

How did I choose these particular memories to be placed in the book? Frequency of recollection. Sometimes a subject simply emerges and then goes away, while others stay a long time. And often, a memory somehow latches and remains there to be studied from all angles. There is a permanence that can be ascribed to it. I considered those memories that met either of these expectations—occurring frequently or somehow latching—to be qualified for inclusion in my memoir.

My approach in writing this book was to present a memory as an essay. I ask the reader to accept each essay as part of a literary mosaic. It is my intent that after getting an expanded impression from the mosaic essays, the reader will have a clear image of each event included—whether it be war or something peaceful. In this way, realistic understanding can emerge through a combination of varied inputs.

Of all the tribulations I experienced as a child, every single one of them can be tied to a war—a bad happening started by someone else. Events like this, I came to understand, were not just happening to me. No, they were all part of a larger event—a world at war—and I was only a small part of a much bigger picture. Thus, when I recap in my memoir a war story about a Thunderbolt pilot who goes to the tail of his plane to barf up his breakfast as part of his walk-around inspection, I am once again a six-year-old kid on the other side of the world who is wondering, *Why do these things happen to only me and my family?* These seemingly unrelated stories reassure me that wars create difficult situations for others as well, and I have included them in order to share this perspective with my readers.

Seven of the many war stories I have collected over the years have been included in this book, the most recent from my son CW4 James Reece Oliver, who spent eight months in the Iraq War. Because of the sincerity and spontaneity with which they were told me, I immediately believed the tellers. Most of them came from military sources, although some did not. All of them were conveyed to me in the first person, just as they were witnessed by their sources.

None of the war stories were simply heard and collected as other people spoke of them. Instead, their sources participated in them, and they form an important portion of the mosaic. I convey them to you as I heard them told me. I heard most of these war stories when I was a junior military officer. I listened to them and accepted their validity because of the consistency of the details in them and the passion of those who told the stories.

In several locations throughout my mosaic of mini-essays, I have chosen to acknowledge individuals and events that have been important influences in my life. I wish to share with readers a description of these situations that represent the values I cherish in this world, thus demonstrating that my thoughts are not only about war.

Author's Statement

I am a voluntarily retired lieutenant colonel in the Regular Air Force component of the US Air Force. My twenty-four years of active duty included participation in the launch of four Minuteman test intercontinental ballistic missiles (ICBMs). I retired in 1984 as commander of the Ninetieth Organizational Missile Maintenance Squadron (90 OMMS), an ICBM maintenance squadron of the Strategic Air Command.

All information contained here is unclassified. For privacy reasons, names of certain individuals have been changed or omitted altogether. In order to convey a communication, I prefer to paraphrase in lieu of the exact words spoken. (In most cases, so many years have passed that I can't remember the exact words spoken anyhow.) I also use paraphrasing so readers can quickly interpret what the speaker of the words meant. I have lived or witnessed most of the events described in this work.

Lt. Col. James S. Oliver, USAF (Ret.)

Acknowledgments

My mama and papa sacrificed their dreams to give their four kids a fair chance to experience and develop opportunities in their lives (such as being able to write this memoir and the book of short stories preceding it). I am grateful to them for their efforts to make certain we four kids survived WWII and adjusted to our social environment after the war. I have often wondered how I could have become a tranquil seventy-eight-year-old now and achieved such a peaceful life without their vision and help. Each time I have studied the tranquility of my environment, I have easily concluded it wouldn't be so without their early guidance and decisions. Bless them both.

Louise Kuhn Oliver is my dear wife, who married me for the long term. She directly assisted in organizing and formatting pages and computer files. Her typing support was invaluable. I literally could not have completed the manuscript without her assistance.

Fé Rebecca (Becky) Oliver died in 2007 of breast cancer. My younger sis told me that if I procrastinated much longer, my memories would be lost to the world forever. In giving me her admonition, she helped develop this book far more than she could have imagined.

Eddie and Manolo were twelve-year-old Filipino friends of the family who assumed responsibility for the survival of our little family toward the end of WWII in the Philippines. They became our guides, protectors, and mentors in a nighttime trek through the jungle to the refugee village of Kawá-Kawá. Their courageous efforts ensured we lived, while they both died at the hands of the enemy. It is because of their sacrifices that I had the opportunity to go on with my life and to collect the memories I've recorded in the chapters that follow.

Robert (Bob) Philip Oliver is the eldest of us four Oliver siblings. Over the years, I have received very meaningful input from my elder brother. In many different ways, he taught me qualities of leadership and, especially, how to prevail. As I grew up, Bob was not only my boss but my leader as well. In so many ways, he was of significant influence—not only in my maturation but also in the writing of this book.

Winston Reece Oliver, my younger brother, and his wife, Carol, have made extensive important contributions to the development of my memoir. Through her questions, Carol has been invaluable in bringing out details I might have missed. At the same time, Winston is a natural historian who has remained in the area of our Oliver family Corners Farm near Akron, Indiana, for many years and has carefully watched over boxes of memorabilia, legal documents, and a variety of reference materials. These have been a great help to me in my writing effort and have steered my writing toward greater accuracy. Also, he has provided me the bulk of translation assistance, because I have been remiss in keeping current in Tagalog language translation skills.

The muse for my secular needs and the guardian angel for sacred necessities—my forever companions—have contributed to my entire life many times and in many ways. I acknowledge their constancy as well as the continuation of their charters to keep me out of trouble. They have watched over me since I was a baby, at which time they were assigned to take care of me. Inasmuch as I am now in my late seventies, they both have done their jobs superbly well. Several times in my life, they have heard me call for help, and they have always responded without hesitating for even a moment. Mostly they just check in with me before I even realize that I require guidance or that I need their assistance. Several times they have given me their rationale: "We help you because you have demonstrated that you don't simply call for us just because we're always available. No, you call when you really need help."

Publication credit goes to the staff members of iUniverse who were assigned to follow my progress—Kathi Wittkamper, Mars Alma, Traci (Mother Hen) Anderson, Lester Diaz, and Michael Janney. Early in the writing process, Traci was available for advice in the many changes of weather an author experiences. Mars has the reassuring patience necessary to her job as check-in coordinator between iUniverse and would-be published authors such as me. She was able to perform miracles in rescheduling my ever-changing milestones for electronic transfer of this manuscript. Soon after the manuscript was accepted by iUniverse, Kathi was on the scene to encourage our continuing efforts with skilled professionalism and useful explanations during our telephone conversations. She explained the editing her company offered, what it would take to make our book "come alive," and the efforts each of us had to take in order to make our book a potential best seller. So many years past, Lester showed me how to find specific references among the various reference books comprised by the library of iUniverse. More than that, his birthplace is Cagayan de Oro, a city on the north coast of Mindanao where long ago much of the Japanese troop action told of early in this book took place.

Introduction

The Japanese bombed Pearl Harbor, and eight hours later they invaded Davao City, Mindanao, Philippines, where I was living with my mama, papa, and three siblings. Therefore, December 7, 1941, also marks the beginning of my personal involvement in three US wars. Note that I was only a preschooler on Mindanao, the southernmost island in the archipelago of the Philippines, when Japanese troops invaded the islands after they had hammered the US naval fleet in Pearl Harbor, Hawaii. Four years later, which seemed a very long time, Japanese troops were finally gone, childhood stressors had been removed, and the Oliver family was reunited with our father, who had come out of the jungle after four years of absence.

My first war, then, was World War II (see chapter 2), which dramatically changed our peaceful comfortable lifestyle into one of confusion, horror, and an intense fight for survival. At that young age, I officially earned the status of prisoner of war, along with my mother and siblings. Four years of my memories of this era, no matter how ugly, are described within. When the war was over in 1945, I was eight and a half years old, with nothing gained and with an everlasting recollection of what a decaying human body smells like. A reader may wonder why I would find it necessary to include such experiences. The answer lies in how they were eventually integrated into my childhood development. There are a number of memories from those years that played an important part in my development from a child into an adult warrior.

Second, I was a participant in the Cold War (see chapter 4) beginning in 1960, when I graduated from Purdue University in West Lafayette, Indiana, and Mama pinned on my commissioning bars as a second lieutenant in the US Air Force. In 1984, I retired after twenty-four years of service as squadron commander of the 90 OMMS in Cheyenne, Wyoming, with a USAF rank of lieutenant colonel.

Third was the Vietnam War (see chapter 6), which I experienced in 1970–1971 at Fort Bragg, North Carolina, and as province psychological warfare advisor for the province of Hau Ngia, Vietnam.

Also featured in my memoir are civilian recollections and explanations from the in-between periods prior to and after WWII, the Cold War, and the Vietnam War (see chapters 1, 3, 5, and 7).

A Family Legacy

Papa—Reece Augustus (Gus) Oliver (1891–1966): According to Indiana State archives and Fulton County historical documentation, I am the great-great-great-great-grandson of Samuel Lane, a Revolutionary War veteran, whose gravesite in an Akron, Indiana, cemetery is marked with a special designation by a local chapter of the Daughters of the American Revolution (DAR).

After a month of travel by oxcart from Akron, Ohio, our earliest relatives arrived at a spot in the woods of what was then the Indiana Territory. According to local historical documents, the leader of the wagon train said in a voice loud enough for everyone to hear, "This is the place!" Records show that Akron, Indiana, was founded on the spot indicated by the leader in 1836.

These earliest of relatives arrived in Akron, which at the time was a small settlement in the Indiana Territory, shortly after the small town was founded in 1836. Several generations later, with the usual name changes through marriage, there is information in local historical documentation that the Oliver family was living about three miles east of the city, at the intersection of Indiana State Road 14 and a turnoff to Rock Lake. Originally known as Oliver's Corner, the agricultural area of about sixty-five acres eventually assumed a more generic name: the Corners Farm. The original homestead burned to the ground and was replaced in generally the same location by my grandparents. This is where Gus (my father) grew up with his three brothers and one sister (Cecil, Ira, Kenneth, and elder sister Densie). He attended school in Akron, Indiana, and graduated from high school in 1910. He was a good student, always loved learning, and began a career as a dedicated teacher in nearby one-room schools the very next year after his high school graduation. In fact, some previous classmates of his were then his students. Each summer he took classes at Indiana University–Bloomington to achieve required certifications necessary to his job as a teacher, after the fact.

In 1920, the US government was looking for young teachers willing to be employed in the Philippines for a monthly salary. This package included payment for round-trip transportation home to the United States every three years. Gus signed up without hesitation. He jumped at the chance to find adventure outside of his little hometown in northern Indiana. He earned a salary that enabled him to teach part of the year, be an enthusiastic adventure seeker, and also send funds home to help his widowed mother.

Once in the Philippines, and with an innate ability to overcome language difficulties, Gus quickly progressed from being a principal to a position as regional school superintendent. In between the school years, he could be found traveling to interesting destinations around the world by such means as tramp steamers and other innovative means of transportation. The stories of his adventures were endless and amazing; I still think of my papa as the original explorer and tomb raider—one who could laugh at five-thousand-year-old curses!

Mama—Flora Carbonell (1900–1986): Unfortunately, in sharp contrast to the Oliver side of my family, we know very little of Mama's Filipino-Spanish Carbonell roots in the Philippine Islands. She told me she was born in Iloilo, on the island of Panay. She also told me her family has a historic background that goes back to the Castile region of Spain and includes tales of Magellan in the Philippines in AD 1500. We do know that a Spaniard named Carbonell was involved with Datu Lapu-Lapu and some local politicians when Magellan was killed with a spear on Mactan Island. When we acted interested in such information, Mama used to wave her hands and remind us all that those events happened hundreds of years ago. Even though we kids were interested, the subject was effectively dropped, and as a consequence we know very little of Mama's historical background

Like our papa, Mama was a dedicated educator, and around 1930 she was appointed supervisor of teaching schools in southern Mindanao, Philippines. She was from a wealthy family. She lived in a fine home that she owned in Davao City and had sophisticated musical preferences for symphonies and operas. Her investments included a second home in the city, at 306 Tiongko Avenue, just two blocks from the home we lived in when the war started, and a small plantation of 110 acres named Catalunan Pequeño (Little Catalonia) a few miles into the country from the city of Davao.

While working at the schools in Iloilo, Gus, the adventurer-educator, met petite and fascinating Flora. They shared a mutual passion for education, and in 1933 they traveled to the United States for further studies of their own. Gus took classes at Indiana University, while Flora earned her master's degree in English at the University of Chicago. Before returning to the Philippines, they managed to circumnavigate the world, and Flora experienced firsthand what it was like to be a partner with Gus and his adventurous ideas.

In 1934, Gus and Flora were married in Davao City. All four of their children were born in the Philippines, with US citizenship—since Papa was a US citizen from Indiana. At that time, the Philippines was still a US possession. They began raising their family during relatively peaceful prewar times in a refined residence on Mapa Street, close to the administrative center of Davao City.

Robert Philip Oliver (b. 1935): (Bob's middle name refers to an early king of Spain; note that it is spelled with only one *l*.) A few years after I was born, Bob became the head of household, a term in the Spanish-oriented culture in which we grew up that meant all major decisions were on his shoulders simply because he was, at the time, the oldest male in the family. At my young age, even I could tell that he had a great deal of responsibility but very little authority—Mama retained that. Even after we moved from the Philippines to Akron, Indiana, Bob remained my mentor, by my choice. I simply looked up to him as a source of wisdom—mostly because he was two years older. Besides, he always seemed to have answers to my many questions.

James Stanley Oliver (b. 1937): (My middle name refers to Stanley Baldwin, who in 1937 was a retiring British prime minister). Curiosity has always been a characteristic of mine. I don't know that I have to correct or adjust anything in order to get rid of the trait. Suffice it to say that I am just curious—especially about something to be yet discovered. Then, when I have an answer, I also want to explain it to someone. That is why I'm also known to be a teacher (probably the result of my Oliver heritage). It is difficult for me to understand that others might not find my discoveries as meaningful and fascinating as I find them to be. I find it very exciting to learn new information about almost anything. One of the best parts about retirement is having more time available to research and understand details of various subjects.

Fe' Rebecca Oliver (1939–2007): Becky was named after her paternal grandmother, Faye Rebecca Hively. After graduating from Beaver Dam High School, Becky moved to New York City, where she became a student of modern dance and studied with Martha Graham. Later she married and lived in San Juan, Puerto Rico, where she earned a BA degree from International University. In later years, she lived in Sacramento, California, continued graduate classes at the University of California–Davis, and was certified to teach English as a second language (ESL). In her later years, she became very interested in Far Eastern medicine and nutrition and was studying to gain certification. Becky cherished her many friends from around the world. She died of breast cancer in August 2007.

Winston Reece Oliver (b. 1941): (He was named after Winston Churchill and our papa.) After graduating from Akron High School, Winston remained in the local area. His two big brothers and sister were already living far from home, and he had an important role in assisting our aging parents with the demands and responsibilities of keeping the farm functioning. He eventually moved to Fort Wayne, Indiana, and was employed by a local division of a large corporation that manufactured jet engines for military and commercial aircraft. He was assigned to a quality control department. Only a two-hour drive from the Corners Farm, he made frequent visits to assist our mama however he could. He drove her places, ran needed errands, and just kept up with her needs as much as he possibly could. I am forever grateful to my little brother for providing the kind of ongoing support for our mama that I was unable to do myself.

Chapter 1

In Between: The Early Years

Davao City and Mindanao

Mama often told me that I couldn't have remembered events that I occasionally recounted to her, because in her mind, I was just too young to remember them. She was skeptical that I would remember events from those "too-young days." Perhaps, she often offered, I had simply heard specific stories from someone else and, over the passing of time that stretched into many years, I had somehow reinforced details enough to be convinced I had lived or witnessed such happenings. I discounted her explanations, however. Now recent research has shown that some kids start remembering early, while others recollect events at a much later stage of their lives, the latter of which is probably more common.

I remember well that Mama used to shout this epithet at us when we kids were young and grubby from playing outside: "You kids look like the skimmings of hell." We knew then that she had been momentarily frustrated by our activities and resulting unacceptable appearance. Now, if her premise is correct about me remembering later childhood events, not the early ones, how could I remember her observation of events that occurred before the war? Remember: I was born in 1937, so when Japanese troops invaded and occupied Davao City, Philippines, where we lived, I was only four and a half years old.

Marciana was a helper to our mama and also a nanny to us kids. Without her help, our whole tenure in Davao City would have been a bad deal, and likely our family would not have survived the war. When I was a child, she removed the scab from an old wound on my knee, perhaps generated a month before through some antic that kids of that age attempt. "It will heal faster," she told me, but the process of removing the scab hurt, and taking advantage of a childhood situation, I managed to create a picture of pain and discomfort accompanied by large tears.

As soon as the scab was removed, a passing fly immediately assumed ownership of the wound. Of course I shooed it away, but it was pesky and returned. I remember killing it with two hands, much as if I were clapping, because as Papa had shown me, two hands are much better than a quick overhead slap. No matter how quick one's hand is, a fly will jump sideways from under a slapping hand because it has pressure sensors on its back. Thus, a fly can tell when an object, such as a descending open hand, is above it. But it doesn't have sensors on its sides. That's a simple explanation of why a fly will invariably escape a downward whack with a flat hand but won't escape when two hands exert pressure upon its sides, which have no sensors. That is the secret of success in killing a fly: use two hands. I learned all this from my papa while I was just a young kid.

During my childhood development, I expressed frustration and anger with temper tantrums, during which I would pound my forehead on anything that was hard. Marciana used to commiserate with me, but Mama would laugh at my antics. I could hear her in the next room, stating, "Maybe he will pound some sense into his head!" Of course, that response would drive me to continue my childhood tantrums more vigorously. Excellent candidates included the hardwood floor and our wood table, the legs of which ended with hand-carved paws of a very large jungle cat. My papa once told me that the table was of narra wood from the interior of the Philippines and that the wood was the hardest and toughest in the world. I think he was right about narra wood.

Many years later, but still a youngster, I one day discovered a chunk of narra and attempted to drive a small new nail into it with a hammer. The nail bent and did not go into the wood; its fibrous grains are situated too close together to allow a foreign object, such as the point of the nail, to enter the space between them. Of course there exists a good probability that the youth in me was trying to prove a point, but I am convinced that narra is the toughest wood in the world.

Books and the Sunday comic pages were a fascination for me even before I could read them myself. One of my early memories from the colorful Sunday comics is lying on the floor and learning about a young girl and her friend, a mouse. She would speak magic words whenever she wished to join the small world of her friend, a mouse with a name and human characteristics who lived in a nice home of his own. I recall that I always wanted to join the girl and her mouse friend because I thought the mouse could possibly be a good friend for me too. The mouse was always dressed up and I thought he would be a wonderful partner for me to play with. Of course, the face of the little girl—human, huge, and startling—would appear on the other side of a windowpane in the mouse's home. She would be looking inside to see if her mouse friend was at home, and if so, she would speak her magic words: "Puff, puff, piffle!" and she would become small like the mouse. Marciana or Mama were reading these types of children's stories to us and sharing the Sunday newspaper comic pages in the days before my idealistic world crashed as a Japanese soldier's boots hammered up the back stairs and then kicked in the kitchen door at the start of WWII in Davao City. (But that's a story for chapter 2.)

On a Typically Hot Day

I once shared with Marciana an early incident I remembered, and she told me I would have been about fifteen months old when I experienced the details I related to her. Our black cars were traveling in a convoy from our Mapa/Jacinto home where we lived in Davao City to our farm. I must diverge a moment to explain—Mama often called the farm Catalunan Pequeño (literally "Little Catalonia"). I now think she did so because our farm was considerably smaller when it was compared to the one adjacent to it, which was named Catalunan Grande.

Much later during the war, we renamed our farm from Catalunan Pequeño to Sunny Brook Farm because of Becky, my little sister. "Becky" was a shortened name for her long name, which was "Rebecca," but we kids called her by her short name all the time. She was a toddler when Mama changed the name of the farm. I remember Mama saying to us, "Our doing that shouldn't confuse anyone." We kids were not confused at all, and we nodded our heads in agreement, fully knowing that to express something along the line of disagreement would be a simple waste of time—at least where our mama was concerned.

Mama insisted on changing the name of the farm to Sunny Brook because it had more meaning to everyone. After all that, she went on to explain that we also had a creek that ran through our farm. Well, yes, that was so if we wanted to call the runoff from Mount Apo a brook. "Remember," she added, "ours is two words: 'Sunny' and 'Brook,' not the same as the title of the popular story [which used only one word—'Sunnybrook']." To us, her argument was valid all the way.

Now back to the story that I recounted to Marciana. I remember our two black cars stopping. The drivers got out of the cars, but Mama, Marciana, and I remained seated in the back of one of the cars. We had stopped near a banana plant grove close to the main entrance of the dirt track leading to our farm, where the track connected to the rudimentary road that led to the huts and shacks of Mintal, a small town about a quarter of a mile away. There was some shouting, and then one of our laborers (synonymous with "tenant" and "*tao*" and "campesino") came out of the local jungle growth and went to the small group near the cars. Evidently he had been running back to the parked cars with a message, because he had drops of sweat on his forehead.

I must have been getting fussy, because Marciana reacted quickly. Two bottles of milk were ready for me, and I immediately drank them. Papa grabbed a rifle from one of the cars and followed the adults into the jungle and disappeared. I probably drank my milk too fast or something, because I remember vomiting all the milk onto my chest and making a mess.

I also remember the mungo beans that grew on our farm. They were about the size of a BB. These beans were boiled and made into a soup that tasted similar to split pea soup. Mungos were a staple of our household.

One Sunday morning, Mama took me to church along with my brother Bob. Papa stayed at home because he had projects to work on. While we were at church, the priest was berating the audience about some issue. I studied his face and his actions. He was an angry man!

"Mama," I said aloud, "I think the priest is angry at us." All around us, members of the congregation twittered and pointed and made comments to one another about my wisdom. I basked in the attention and then did silly things like pick my nose. The next Sunday when they went to church,

I was left behind with my dedicated father, who always worked at home on Sundays. I was miffed that the family group simply went to church without once consulting me.

Screams in the Middle of Night

When I was less than four years old, bedtime was literally a nightmare for me because I would invariably wake up screaming in fear. In the process I would wake up the entire household. In my nightmares, a fearsome cleaning woman would have caught me and sunk her hands into my chest. Or she would be hiding in a dark corner, just waiting for me to drift off to sleep; then I would be vulnerable to her murderous attack—and so would the entire household, because I then wouldn't be able to warn anyone that after she was done with me, she would come after them, one by one! Every little child has a monster that hides under the bed. My monster happened to have more human features than other monsters. Mine always wore a white cleaning apron, and I could never see her malevolent face because it was always hidden under a fold of her white cleaning bonnet.

She would search the hallways for me, locate my bed, and creep up on me during the night while I was sleeping to do me great harm of some sort. I would drift off to sleep again knowing that soon she would sneak up on me and get her claws into my chest.

While awake, I would perspire profusely while looking into the terrorizing darkness, wondering what corner she had discovered she could hide in until I drifted off to sleep once more. I would become vulnerable to her attack after I fell asleep. Her sudden rush at me would be unstoppable, and I would wake up and scream, waking up the whole household in the process.

Much later, I analyzed that blood rushing through my vascular system was under such pressure that its incessant pounding in my head exactly matched the sounds of her footsteps. Just hearing her footsteps get closer and closer terrified me all the more, and my system would pump blood faster and faster until even my eardrums would feel my blood rushing past them. My eardrums would roar, of course. It all meant to me that she had somehow located me in the darkness and I was vulnerable once more because I had fallen asleep. Actually, I had generated a closed-loop fear mechanism: my heart began pounding whenever I would conjure up the image of my monster—the cleaning woman. Also, the more intensely my heart would beat, the closer her footsteps came to me. And when I thought she had missed finding me, of course the intensity of my heartbeat would lessen and then I would no longer have an inclination to scream. I didn't carry this childhood habit into my adult years, thank goodness.

It wasn't until many years later, after retiring from the US Air Force more than thirty years ago, that I finally came to terms with my early childhood nightmares. Louise and I were walking through an annual festival in Larkspur, Colorado, one fine summer day when I noticed a discarded container of household cleanser. I recognized it immediately. There was a cleaning lady on the can, her face completely obscured by her white-winged cleaning cap. I realized this was the image I had found so frightening as a child. She was the horrifying culprit who had caused my frequent nightmares. I was amazed when I recognized the icon of the faceless cleaning woman on the side of this discarded cleanser can. Brazen and bold in the daylight, there was my childhood nemesis! Finally I knew who my nighttime stalker was, and she was faceless as always, except she was much more acceptable to me because I had also grown to adulthood.

This little excursion about twenty years ago gave me an opportunity to review most of the factors associated with the causes of my screams in the middle of the night when I was a child. Finally I was able to dismiss the thought of her, and the faceless cleaning lady who had terrified me when I was a youngster finally went away forever.

Like many young families, we had special words we learned to use, mostly regarding the bathroom and other personal issues. Urine was *boo*, and *moots* were encrustations we occasionally found around our eyes and nostrils when we woke up in the mornings. Fecal matter was *oh-ho*, probably from earlier sessions with potty training in which an accident occurred, resulting in a child's assessment of the entire episode as "uh oh!" Yes, even at the age of seventy-eight, I still use my childhood euphemisms. Need I write more?

The Spider in the Bathroom

I found the bathroom spider terrifying. It just plainly terrified me. Why our mama thought it was such a beautiful thing, I'll never know. The spider was black, very large, and hairy, and it tended to stay in a corner of the bathroom. I saw it move just a little at times, and each time it did, I was prepared to run toward the kitchen and more light. I learned many years later that it was a species of tarantula. It had somehow wandered into the white-tiled bathroom.

Actually, the light color of the stone tiles might have made the spider seem huge in my eyes, but much later, I concluded the spider was so large that it stayed in the bathroom because it was just too big to crawl under the bathroom doors during the night. I once came into the bathroom but could not find the spider. I froze and could not move—until I was able to locate the large black hairy thing once more in a far corner toward the window.

I concluded it was trying to find a way out of its confinement and had moved toward the source of light. I would sit on the stool but in the process keep an eye on the spider, ready to jump and run to the closed door if it moved. Mama had sternly told us to leave it alone because it ate insects. She was quite stern about it, so we kids heeded her warning.

One time I was using the toilet in the bathroom when the spider moved. I saw the movement and almost screamed. Whenever I had to use the bathroom, I always looked for the spider before making any move toward the toilet.

Music, Poetry, and Mama

I still remember some of the songs Mama used to sing to herself when I was a young child before the war. They were the common verses all young children understand, with directions to clap hands, stamp feet, or reach up to the sky, with perky little rhymes and rhythms that fascinate and make everyone think the world is a magical, wonderful place. Most of the ones I remember best are the same ones enjoyed by youngsters all around the world.

One song I heard from Mama before and after the war was a Thanksgiving tribute. It always impressed me that the words were written by a religious reformer hundreds of years earlier but they still had meaning for me.

Not everything Mama shared with us was musical. She seemed to have memorized many powerful poetic stanzas from the classical greats. I was too young at the time to really understand the words and their originally intended meanings. I definitely was left with the intended emotions and could draw my own conclusions based on where we were as Mama recited the powerful words to us. She probably was also doing it for her own purposes of trying to maintain a sensible existence when things all around us were not very encouraging.

I was three or four years old, and I still remember many of these lines. I had so many questions about them, and I was probably a pesky preschooler asking questions all the time. There just were not enough hours each day to answer them all. But then the war broke out, and we were often reminded by our mama that we needed to be thinking more about what it would take to survive.

The Neighborhood

Our next-door neighbors were evidently Spaniards with backgrounds in education. Mr. Santos had been tasked with something to do with schools. Inasmuch as Spain had owned the Philippines archipelago before it was awarded to the United States, Spain was previously responsible for educating the populace. How best to do this? Send a Spaniard with a background in education, of course. (During my childhood, the United States "owned" the Philippines, having received it as a wartime reparation from Spain, and was therefore responsible for educating its population.)

Evidently also an opera lover, Mrs. Santos was a kitchen singer. The opera arias she sang in a falsetto voice were obscure to me. Besides knowing the words of many operas, she also was skilled at playing the piano. Mama would mock her singing by practically yodeling the same tunes she sang. Our opera-singing neighbor and mocking mama could be heard all over the neighborhood, and I was embarrassed. I mentioned this to Mama, but how important is embarrassment to a four-year-old? She disregarded my concern. I am not really a devotee of opera, yet to this day, opera music is very meaningful to me in many ways; it always reminds me of Mama in those early childhood years.

I always found the loud voice of our neighbor, the wannabe kitchen opera singer, offensive. The entire neighborhood could hear both the would-be opera star's voice, followed by our mama's mocking yodel very soon afterward. Then Mrs. Santos would suddenly become quiet. Mama would become quiet. The whole neighborhood would become quiet, much as if they were waiting for another shoe to drop.

Bob was my leader, so I religiously followed him when he decided that we were going to get even with Mrs. Santos. According to my way of thinking at that age—which was perhaps four years old—anyone could tell that Mama had in some way been offended because she would start yodeling opera arias all by herself, without bring goaded into doing so by an irksome neighbor. In fact, she was able to yodel so loudly at those times that all the neighbors could easily hear her. Again, I passed on these observations to Mama, who simply nodded. So much for the input of a four-year-old!

Wearing short white pants, Bob and I slyly crossed under the fenced alleyway under the watchful eye of Old Blabbermouth and Tell-All herself (Mrs. Santos), and we then pulled up seedlings from our neighbor's garden. Afterward, feeling somewhat like the mouse that ate all the cheese, I tried to be cool about a situation that had somehow surfaced over Mrs. Santos' garden. Our Mama observed, "Oh, goodness, but where did you get the dirt that you streaked across the pockets of your white pants?"

I managed to stammer out some paltry excuse. You see, I was just learning to tell the truth always and to never tell a lie. But she was extremely angry with Bob! He tried to lie his way out of his predicament as easily as I had lied out of mine, but she would have none of it! "I want you to remember that you are two years older than he is!" she yelled at him.

Even at that age, I kept asking myself, *How could she know? How did she find out?* It seems to me that radio news of a big war started about then, and the garden escapade was somehow forgotten.

Billy lived across the street from us. He had red hair and a freckled face and was very pale. He was only a boy, a typical American kid. I had already stereotyped him. My brother Bob discovered that by using a broken piece of mirror, he could reflect a beam of sunlight into Billy's eyes. At the time, when Bob was explaining the physics of this endeavor to me, he told me that doing this would cause the person targeted to become nauseated. I believed that piece of sage knowledge years afterward. So from then on, I knew that anyone who looked at reflected light, light emitted from a welding torch, or sparks from a grinder for too long would become nauseated to the extent that he would want to vomit.

A Swarm of Grasshoppers

The grasshoppers all of a sudden materialized; only God knows where they came from. It was midmorning when we first started noticing that greenish grasshoppers (of course, some may have been more brownish in color) were starting to show up in the unlikeliest of places. Then, all of a sudden, they were everywhere. Mama would open the empty pantry and two or three grasshoppers at a time would fly out, startling her and anyone else nearby.

Deeply introspective even at such an early age, I studied myself closely, thinking maybe I did something wrong to warrant such a thing. I felt guilt for doing something wrong to warrant such an event, and even as early in my life as I was, I just knew that such a pestilence had been called down by God because I had done something wrong. Had I already become evil? I was only four and a half years old, but I concluded that even youngsters can be bad. I felt that until I sorted everything out, maybe I should continue to stay close to my mama only, and no one else.

The insects flew in by the millions, so thick at times that the noonday sun was blotted out by swarm upon swarm of them. The skies would become clear, and then suddenly the sun would be blotted out once more. Looking back on this grasshopper event, I am of the opinion that in all the history of mankind, there has been no swarm of grasshoppers that blotted out the sun so much that everything became pitch-black or made surroundings so dark that a person could not distinguish the identity of people near or about. After all, light is always reflected from distant fields and foothills. While surroundings may become darker than usual in daylight, nothing becomes so indistinct that people experience nighttime. Such happenings are merely figments of writers' imaginations.

Some of the locals were pretty innovative about the nuisance of the grasshopper swarm. They were resourceful in quickly setting up hot food stands, replete with small cans of hot cooking oil—usually from coconuts grown in the abundant groves all about. (This condition of abundant coconuts was to change in a matter of days.) I thought the process fascinating.

I adopted a local chef and followed him around to the sidewalk intersection that he had selected for his stand—I suppose because in that location there would be more customers for his cookery. The process was fairly simple: out of the millions upon millions of grasshoppers all about us, an unlucky one would land on the grass or a nearby bush, and then the chef's quick hands would pick it up and deftly throw it into a can of boiling oil. Very soon he would use a bamboo spatula to fish out the grasshopper before it turned dark brown, and it was then offered to a customer. For a few coins, the customer would accept the crunchy morsel, pop it in his mouth, and go on his way.

Early on I was offered a taste, but I politely declined because I remembered some warning from Mama about diseases and stomachache. Even then I was already creating what I would later call the invisible leash. With the invisible leash, a person can be a thousand miles distant from his guiding source of right or wrong and yet make morally correct decisions—just as if a source or guiding light is standing right next to him.

The idea behind the development of the invisible leash is that a source of guidance—such as my mama—would be standing beside me and would always respond correctly to the question, what should I do now? The situation speaks to availability of the source—but what's to be done if the source is not available? Well, that is where the invisible leash comes in. And it behooves an individual to soon learn a need for such a thing.

Anyway, my brother and I chased green grasshoppers most of the afternoon. Then, at sunset, we went to our new home to sleep. When we woke up the next day, the grasshoppers were gone. But in the hot sun, we did smell their carcasses for several days after. Eventually the unpleasant smell also went away.

* * *

11

Raul O. Tolentino has been the US Oliver family legal representative in Davao City, Mindanao, Philippines, for almost forty years. He added a story of his own to the war stories collection. He grew up as I did, a young schoolboy living through the terrors of World War II and the Japanese occupation of Davao City and the Philippines homeland. Indeed, it is a wonder that we survived at all. What a giant step he made from the witnessing as an eleven-year-old boy of two vicious decapitations of two suspected guerilla activists by Japanese occupation military forces, to recently celebrating his eighty-first birthday. I appreciate the conversations I have had with Raul, which verified for me the tone of the populace in the postwar Philippines. Evidently his mother knew my mama, and I felt a special bond with him although we never knew each other in our youthful years. I've appreciated being able to occasionally have this direct contact in our later years.

Attorney Tolentino shares my recognition in this memoir with journalist, historian, and scholar Ernesto I. Corsino, also from Davao City, whose diverse works have been helpful references for me and are frequently cited by Philippine historians and academicians alike.

Chapter 2

World War II: Times Not for Kids

Japanese Military Occupation of Davao City

Papa was in the interior of Mindanao when Japanese warplanes bombed the Davao City administrative buildings just a few blocks away from our family home, within eight hours after they had completed a surprise strike against Pearl Harbor, Hawaii. Mama and her four young kids were living in our Mapa Street home in Davao City, Mindanao, Philippines.

Initially, Papa had been sent away from his home in Davao City to inspect all 127 schools he had established throughout the island of Mindanao on behalf of the Philippine government and the US Department of Education. In a statement compiled in 1955, he describes these responsibilities: "I was an Acting Division Superintendent of Schools for the province of Agusan. I was an employee of the Bureau of Education of the Philippine Government for about 26 years prior to the Japanese invasion of the Philippines. On 9 December 1941, I received a telegram from the Director of Education to close all schools of the Division (approximately 127 schools) and await further instructions. I have never received further instructions." (Readers should be aware that whenever I refer to the Philippine government before WWII, most program funding came from the United States. After the war, the Republic of the Philippines gained its independence, so from 1946 on, the budget for education programs became the responsibility of the new government of the Philippines.)

Early in the Japanese occupation of Davao City, Mindanao, we were evicted from our family home, which was taken over by the Japanese military. We moved into another nearby property; in fact, it was just across the alley. Threatened with starvation, we moved once again from the second city home to our ranch farm, Catalunan Pequeño, which we renamed Sunny Brook Farm on Mama's guidance.

The war lasted four years, and several terrors accompanied each of those years. For many years I could not even write about that time. As a father and former squadron commander, I can tell you these years were not good for raising kids.

*   *   *

Approximately midmorning of Monday December 8, 1941, a Japanese warplane dive-bombed the Davao City administration buildings, which were about two blocks from our home. The concussion created by the bombs was incredible. With baby Winston in her arms, Mama called out for us kids who were playing outside to come to her. I was four years old; my older brother, Bob, six; and our little sister, Becky, two. We three came running to our mama.

Mama, who was strict, spoke with unmatched authority. "Into the closet." she commanded. She grabbed pillows from the bed and promptly put them around our ears. She explained, "Keep them on. They'll keep your eardrums from being destroyed." We stayed there until the explosions stopped, and then Mama came to tell us that it was all right to come out of the stifling closet.

When the first bomb struck, the explosion was so loud that my lungs felt as if they would collapse. In later years, I found this to be an amazing impression, because the distance was more than two blocks! During my analysis, I determined that this was the first time I had ever heard an explosion of such power, so the explosion surely could have taken my breath away. Then the plane went away. I remember that Mama stayed close to a radio for a long time and listened to an announcer explain the progress of the Japanese attack.

We did not see or hear from our father again for four years. It was well known that he had been organizing a guerilla operation, the 107th Mindanao Guerilla Division. If he had been discovered with us by the Japanese soldiers, we would all have been killed. This was the beginning of four years of terror and hardship. First came the bombs, and then, a few days later, we received a surprise visit by a Japanese shock trooper.

Shortly after the airplane dive-bombed the nearby city administration buildings, our family was all in the kitchen, on the second floor, when we heard and felt the whole building shake; this was caused by the heavy boots of a Japanese soldier running up the steps to our back door. Mama was cradling baby Winston in her arms. Soon enough, the kitchen door was kicked in.

A Japanese soldier wearing a dark-colored leather skullcap stood in the doorway, holding a rifle with a fixed bayonet extending beyond the barrel of the gun. (Many years later, I learned from books I had read that this was typical headgear of Japanese marines in combat situations.) He shouted something we didn't understand as he stood on the kitchen porch. The Japanese language was indeed a barrier, but we fully knew his intent as he shouted to us and waved the bayonet. I am glad he didn't start shooting immediately, because it was clear he had a finger on the trigger of his rifle. He shouted at us again, but we didn't understand.

The soldier then went to the back bedrooms, and we could hear closet doors opening and clothes being ripped by the point of his bayonet. We could hear his boots and movements as the floorboards of polished wood creaked. Later, after he had gone, we inspected our clothes on their hangers and discovered huge cuts in them. They had been destroyed by bayonet thrusts. I am sure that if anyone, even a child, had been in the bedroom, he or she would have been shot or bayoneted.

Then he came around the corner from the bedrooms and called out to his two compatriots, who were waiting on the front porch just outside the front door—also with bayonets on their rifles and wearing dark leather skullcaps. No one had heard them use the front steps, so I now believe that part of their tactic was to silently position two soldiers at the front door while the other shock trooper charged up the back stairway. If anyone attempted to escape the home, he or she would be shot in the back. I'm certain all three were ready to shoot anyone who made the mistake of fleeing out the front door.

Years later I learned while attending squadron officer school at Maxwell Air Force Base (AFB) in Alabama that shock soldiers such as these are used by the sector commander to get the point across to every family that the city has been invaded.

The soldier inside the house came into the kitchen again. After excitedly shouting to his two compatriots, he motioned with his rifle, all the while shouting at us. Of course we didn't understand what he was saying, so we simply watched and followed his motions and stayed out of the way. He opened the refrigerator door with his left hand and took out two fresh eggs—the other hand holding the trigger of the rifle with its fixed-bayonet pointing directly at us three kids, who huddled around our mama's legs. He flipped the tops off the eggs, and we watched as he swallowed them down raw. He once again shouted something at us, and then he disappeared out the same back door he had just kicked in.

Watching the soldier, I felt a gag reflex in my own throat, and I remember thinking that the man was really hungry to eat whole eggs raw! As young as I was, I nevertheless was impressed with his self-sufficiency and air of confidence, despite the fact that many years later I realized he could have shot us anytime. I also learned later that an egg consumed raw is one of the quickest ways to get protein into one's system. A raw egg provides an energy boost, and the shock soldier would need an energy boost, all right, if he were planning to run up several more back stairways!

For the rest of the day, we could hear occasional shots across the city. We could also hear women's screams.

A few days after the kitchen door was kicked in by the Japanese soldier, three soldiers arrived at our home on Mapa Street. They politely knocked on our front door. We were being evicted! Orders to move were clearly spelled out by an administrative officer from one of the large ships in the bay. The administrative officer was pompous as he stood there. The door was pushed open wide, to clearly show behind him two soldiers armed with rifles and fixed bayonets. He announced to everyone in a loud voice, "This will be the home of the General in charge of the local Imperial Japanese Army. Anyone found in this house after two days will be shot or bayoneted. Soldiers will accompany the residence inspector, and they will kill anyone found here. Do you understand?"

When Mama nodded, we did also. We always followed her lead. I was so small that I couldn't have understood a single word he said, but if my mama agreed to whatever he dictated, that was fine with me.

I knew we had to evacuate our home, and initially I found the whole idea a little exciting. Then, soon enough, I found out that I couldn't just return on a whim. And as matters turned out, never again did I have a chance to return to our home. The very important thing to me was that his orders clearly spelled out that we had to move out of our home as soon as possible. We didn't waste time learning what had to be done.

Mama shouted instructions to us, and we simply followed orders. By her manner and looks, we knew this was a serious situation, and we neither whined nor argued. She rummaged through each of our dressers and picked out what we could wear. All our preparation had to be done within two days. I believe she started by packing provisions for the youngest child, which would have been Winston. He was three months old, only a baby, when the Japanese soldier rudely appeared in our kitchen.

We completed packing and departed the next morning for our new temporary home. Mama made arrangements to move into our nanny's home, which was next door to ours. Once we were settled in, Marciana was able to confirm that some general, a commander of regional Japanese ground forces, was going to take up residence in our evacuated home. Reportedly he had lived a matter of months aboard the flagship of the invading forces, but now his new residence would be on land—in our home. To be honest about it, I wasn't proud of that news. I had no bad feelings about the fact either. I just wished that we had not moved our stuff out of our home just because of him.

*   *   *

Japanese sentries had been posted in their small sentry boxes throughout Davao City, mostly at major intersections where a lot of people crossed or met one another. A good many years later, I learned that after a city has been invaded, part of the education of its population is to ensure that each inhabitant comprehends that the city has been invaded and knows who the invaders are (that is, who is now boss over one's daily social schedule and food supplies, and even one's life itself). The invading Japanese military force in Davao City was able to accomplish this citywide indoctrination in a minimum amount of time through widespread use of sentry boxes. Sentries always stood in their boxes in a military posture best described as a loose attention, and they were always armed with loaded rifles with fixed bayonets.

Every time a person confronted a sentry box, he was expected to stop, turn toward the sentry, and then respectfully bow to him from the waist. It was essential to the passerby that some form of acknowledgment be given by the sentry, such as a nod of the head, a wave of the hand, or some other indication that the sentry had noticed the expected signs of respect. Often a brave city dweller would argue with the soldier that he had already shown him respect by bowing. Just as often, the sentry himself would play games with passersby by shooting them or marching out of his box to bayonet them even though they had already performed as required. This approach of instilling fear was how whole segments of Davao City were subjugated overnight. The idea was to quickly educate everybody that there was a new sheriff in town.

In 1997, I toured a history museum in Hong Kong, China. One exhibit included a Japanese sentry box. I realized in amazement that I had seen one just like it as a child in the Philippines during the WWII occupation by Japanese forces.

*   *   *

One day early in the invasion and eventual occupation of the entire city of Davao by Japanese military forces, Mama and my brother Bob were out in the city somewhere, looking for food for us little ones. Because of innate pride, and perhaps because she was showing her young son that he did not have to bow to a sentry at his young age of six, she did not bow to the sentry. The irate Japanese soldier shouted at her from his sentry box, and according to my brother Bob, she shouted back some filthy words. The sentry may not have understood any English words but he knew what rage was in an individual, and through his gesticulations, he was able to express that he was intent on enforcing a rule that everyone followed: the rule was that everyone who passed by his sentry box had to bow to him. So as he aimed the rifle at her chest. Bob told me later that he thought he was going to be an orphan immediately. Mama was very lucky. Reluctantly, she acquiesced by bowing ever so slightly to the sentry, who then lowered his rifle and waved her and my brother past him.

Bob, the seven-year-old, described to me, the five-year-old, that our mama was angry at a system that required American citizens to bow to Japanese sentries. She was too proud to bow, American citizen or not, yet she was not adept at dodging a sentry in his guard box either. We all knew that everyone who passed a sentry box was to bow in front of it, but one time during a search for food with Bob, Mama decided to avoid the situation altogether by taking a different route. She told him that they would fool the sentry by walking a block out of their way on a different street than usual. A group of soldiers who had been lounging in the shade of a home they had commandeered saw them coming down the street. One of them said something to the others that only they could understand. The group responded with a knowing laugh. Then the one who had made the comment strode out into the street, hit Mama on the side of the face, and shouted at her. She fell to the ground. I heard about this incident when she and Bob arrived back home. I observed and commented that her face was badly swollen.

That afternoon, she and Bob walked many blocks to the Japanese Embassy in Davao City to file a complaint against the soldier who had hit her. Embassy personnel turned the case over to their intelligence officer, who was to call on her at home in a few days.

He came to where we lived. He wore civilian clothes and talked with Mama. She told us that he had gone to school at Harvard University and that she had much in common with him because he had been educated in the United States. So had she, at the University of Chicago, where she earned her master's degree in English. They talked a long while; but I never knew what the final resolutions were.

War Story Number One

This is a war story described to me by Raul O. Tolentino, an attorney still living and working at his law firm in Davao City who represents the Oliver family in the United States in attempts to settle disputes regarding their Philippine properties, as well as to sell those properties.

Having innocently climbed a tree as a kid to get some coconuts, Raul watched as a group of Japanese soldiers began moving into the area directly below him. He knew he had to stay very still to avoid being noticed.

Insects—especially biting black ants—the high humidity, and intense heat of the day started to affect him, but he persevered because he knew he had no choice. Young as he was at the time, he had enough sense to know that his very life depended on staying silent.

After their job was done, the officer and his armed soldier went away. Then Raul was able to climb down without drawing attention. As a seven-year-old kid, he was horrified by what he had just seen. A sword had been used to decapitate two Filipinos who were suspected of being guerillas. But first both young men had been forced to dig a large hole and stand on the edge. When they were decapitated, their heads simply fell off, and each body "leapt" forward into the grave each victim had just dug.

Night Trek with Our Little Red Wagon

Once again we were forced to move from our second home, adjacent to our real home, at Jacinto and Mapa Streets—this time because there was no food in the city. Expressed another way, all Mama's children were starving, and Mama didn't know where the next bite would come from. Already baby Winston's forearm was smaller than the diameter of an adult's little finger.

Marciana, our ever-faithful domestic helper, was with us in the city at that time, and she and Mama would go out daily, looking for something to feed us. They would walk and walk very far throughout the city but would often come back without anything at all. One morning, after several days of fruitless searches for food, Mama told us to pack our clothes and everything we would ever need for a long, long time.

Packing orders didn't mean much to me, and I didn't have much to take along anyway. We hadn't brought much from our real home when the soldiers evicted us, and besides, I wouldn't have known what was mine to pack and what clothes belonged to someone else. Our meager selections—everything that an adult, three growing children, and one three-month-old baby might need—were collected and placed into our children's little red wagon. Mama knew that if we were going to survive, we had to get out of the city.

She told us that we were going to our Catalunan Pequeño farm, about seven miles outside the city. We learned that we would have to walk every step of the way, in the dark of night. Mama emphasized that we could make no noise—especially when she told us to be quiet! We were just kids, so we placed emphasis on the Great Adventure side of it, and looked forward to the excitement of the whole trek—instead of finding fault with the plan.

We started out when the night was so dark we couldn't even tell who was near us by sight, although we knew as soon as the person spoke softly. Recognizing a whispered voice turned out to be very important. Mama carried Winston, the baby, who could only cry. I clearly recall during that nighttime trek in pitch-black from our city home to our farm, we wouldn't have had any problems drawing attention from patrolling Japanese soldiers with baby Winston's crying, because he was so small and weakened from lack of food that he was almost dead anyway. When he cried, his sounds were so tiny; he sounded like a small music box with perforations in all its sides—more like a faint wheeze than a baby's cry. He sometimes cried silently, much like the whispering sound of a breeze blowing through the clumps of cogon that surrounded the city. So the baby would be no problem at all. Besides, he was so small that he looked as if he were part of the bundle of rags used to wrap him for the journey.

Marciana didn't go with us. I think she had friends or relatives in the city. However, a man was with us. I didn't know him, but I think he was Marciana's half brother. He was short and wore black pants and a sweaty white T-shirt that needed to be laundered. I am so grateful, as I write about these early experiences, for individuals such as him, who helped us at the risk of their own lives.

At the edge of the city, we needed to cross over the river on the remnants of the Bankerohan Bridge; however, it had been severely damaged in these early stages of the War, making normal passage questionable. Also, it was being guarded by troops from a nearby Japanese military compound. Sometime after we arrived at the broken bridge, Mama told us kids to stay in the dark with the wagon while she and the man went ahead to the military compound. I fell asleep, and I don't know what negotiations transpired.

Soon we were on our way once more, walking past the compound, picking our way across the damaged bridge, and moving into the blackness again. After what seemed a long, long time, the man picked me up and I was able to sleep as he walked. I liked him, yet I didn't like him. He smelled of tobacco that came through his skin. On the other hand, he was carrying me, and I didn't have to work so hard trying to sleep. Our small group, pulling only the little red wagon of carefully selected personal items, finally arrived at the farmhouse at our Catalunan Pequeño. It was still very dark. I had no way of knowing back then that this would turn out to be our base camp for several years to come.

Settling into Sunny Brook Farm

The farmhouse was not furnished or equipped for use as a home. It was no more than a daytime gathering location where the owners (my parents) would visit from the city to check up on crop conditions, workers, and so on. There were no beds or even mattresses. That first night, all I knew was that at last we could stop walking through the darkness, and all I wanted to do was sleep!

At the farm, Mama simply set about trying to keep us all alive. I don't know what she told my brother Bob to do, especially with us kids, if something went wrong. (Years later I learned that the very start of a war—when the shock troops of an aggressing country first meet a usually recalcitrant community population—is when things may go wrong.)

Soon Mama's breast milk dried up and she lost that valuable source of nourishment for her baby. A very resourceful woman, she often boiled sweet potatoes—*camotes*, the locals called them—which grew naturally on the grounds of the farm. A person needs to know what the leaves looked like, however, before digging for camotes. When they were thoroughly cooked in the coals, she made a mash out of them with a tablespoon. Mama then fed baby Winston with the same large spoon. He was merely a few months of age, but given a choice of food or no food, he quickly learned to eat whatever she could find for him.

Finding food was a continual challenge; we all helped as much as possible. We older boys could trap fish, and Bob became increasingly skilled at building and setting traps to collect birds, lizards. and small rodents that could be cooked for our consumption. This provided some protein to augment the native bananas, oranges, and pomelos we ate. For example, we learned how to find papayas and *gwayabanes*, which are more common, but still wild, fruits. Every now and then, Bob would find *lanzones*, a small, pulpy fruit with a very bitter seed.

In a few days, we settled into simple routines that eventually became almost ritualistic. Just before going to sleep, we would gather in the pitch-blackness to sit cross-legged in a circle at the head of the ladder stair that led to the top floor and bedroom of our farmhouse. Mama would tell us stories and recite Mother Goose rhymes, all in total darkness. We would just slap away the mosquitoes while Mama led us in singing typical childhood songs. I would intently listen to Mama sing opera (even if, as I suspected, she made up some of the words).

At the end of each night's session, we kids would repeat a prayer in unison, and immediately afterward, we heard our mama say the words of each stanza. After a few nights, we had learned the prayer and said it out loud to ourselves (on Mama's orders to us).

*　*　*

Initially, there really was a Sunny Brook at the farm. It was simply a rock-strewn creek, which several years later I learned was a typical stream of water running down the side of a large mountain, such as Mount Apo (a nearby volcano that happens to be the highest mountain in the Philippines). Soon after our arrival to the area, a contingent of soldiers from the Japanese military compound across the river started building a small concrete dam upriver from where we got our daily water. Their center of operations was located in a large warehouse-type building that had a rusted metal roof that was probably made of corrugated iron, like the cover over our farmhouse. They were about one hundred yards up a shallow bank on the other side of the river.

When the builders of the dam started the project, they first had to divert the small river (with no consideration for anyone downriver who depended upon it for drinking, cooking, and washing). Once they started work on the dam, it seemed to me that it took a very long time to complete. I already had in mind that the soldiers were planning to divert the water for their own use. Sure enough, they did. As a consequence, our portion of the little creek went virtually dry.

As it turned out, the complete diversion was short in duration. Nevertheless, our Sunny Brook was never again the same, even after a normal flow of water resumed when the reservoir was filled. Still, the temporary lack of water indicated how vulnerable we were because we were downstream.

*   *   *

Our loyal pet dog Tanny was a farm dog, a mostly-basenji mix. Therefore, he did not bark. As I remember, he was at the farm when we relocated from the city to Sunny Brook Farm and stayed with us during the entire four years of the war. Occasionally Tanny would round the corner of the farmhouse in a big hurry until he found one of us, and he would then wag his tail and practically tug at us to come with him, as if to say, "Hurry, I want you to see what I have just seen."

The one selected by Tanny would follow the dog around the house to the area of the chicken nests, and of course there was nothing there. After a while, we kids and Mama wised up and didn't respond. We realized later that he was trying to warn us about something.

Few things were more sacred than the eggs that our chickens could produce. One time when Tanny led us to the chickens, Mama discovered to her horror that many precious eggs were ruined. Naturally, she blamed the dog. In a rage, she grabbed a *bakyá*—a heavy wooden shoe—from her foot and began beating him. His eyetooth broke off, and the nerve was showing. Later I found the chipped tooth, and I kept it for many years.

I have since read that an egg predator such as a North American raccoon or a North American opossum will tend to scatter eggshells all about a nest, whereas a snake who has ingested an egg will more likely regurgitate eggshells in a clump. Animals don't typically consume the shells because they have no food value; their sole natural function is to be a receptacle for the contents of the egg. I recall seeing three or more clumps—indicating that a snake was the culprit—among the chicken nests that day when Tanny was beaten. Not a single scattering of eggshells do I remember seeing. Poor Tanny—I believe he was beaten for doing his job, which was to keep larger four-legged predators and snakes away from the nests. It was a snake that was eating the eggs. We were later to discover from Bob that it was a king cobra—a large species that is venomous. According to Bob, the snake's head was so high that it looked down on him.

*   *   *

Several days after our nighttime trek with Bob's little red wagon to begin living at Sunny Brook Farm, the intelligence officer from the Japanese Embassy showed up. Bob told me that he was the same intelligence guy from the embassy. Mama was surprised; all of us were surprised. She expressed that she didn't know how he found out we were at the farm. I shouldn't have been surprised, because everyone knew the location of Catalunan Pequeño. I concluded that the man had asked questions and then simply gone where people pointed.

The officer wanted to know if we had seen our dad recently. He took us kids aside, away from Mama, and asked us many questions about our father: "Was it nice seeing your Dad again? How often does he come to visit? When was he here for the last time? Did he bring presents to you?" It was all a cat-and-mouse game.

Our responses were easy and truthful. Of course our father never came to visit. It was obvious that the officer kept Mama apart from us lest we be influenced in our answers to his questions. After a bit, he departed, and we never saw him again. We thought we would see him again, but we never did. I was impressed that the very same officer from the Japanese Embassy in Davao City had come all the way out to the farm to find us.

*   *   *

The farm's nipa hut was built several years earlier by our tenant farmers. This was a small bamboo shelter made of native materials and covered with a grass-thatched roof—a typical structure in remote jungle areas. (I observed what looked to me just like my nipa huts in the Philippines when Louise and I visited an isolated native village on the banks of the Amazon River in Brazil.) Our Sunny Brook Farm nipa hut was located just a few minutes away from the farmhouse, through the jungle undergrowth. We had to eradicate the path that led to it so we could use it as a hiding place if needed. Really, anyone could have found it, but it was better than nothing.

This would at least be a place to hide if Mama thought we were not safe in the farmhouse. Only later did I comprehend that this was my first exposure to the concept of a plan B. We never really talked about it on that level, but we knew that if Mama sensed a dangerous situation, the nipa hut would be our hiding place. Although we kids played around the hut, we all knew to carefully remove any indication of a path that might lead anyone else to the little structure.

Soon after we settled into our Sunny Brook farm, a few months after leaving our new home in Davao City, the tribulations of childhood diseases finally got to us. One day I looked at my fecal stool and it was a tiny plug of mucus material. I told my brother Bob about it. He said that his was the same way. We described this situation to our mama. She allowed that it looked a lot like dysentery to her. Even though we were all dying, we had a long laugh about the whole works, and we continued to treat our childhood diseases like everyday occurrences.

Late one morning I lay down on the ground beside our nearby, hidden nipa hut and fell asleep. Later on, I awoke and mentioned to Bob that I was pretty sick and that perhaps he should go get Mama. She came after a long while. I told her, "Mama, I don't feel so good." This was the end of my conversation. She said, "It's no wonder you feel bad! You are out in the direct heat of the sun. If you are going to die on me, die like an Oliver and get into the shade!"

In a huff, she turned and went away, presumably to the farmhouse. Ashamed, I dragged myself to the shady ground next to the nipa hut. I slept some more, for at least six hours. When I woke up, I was drenched with sweat, and long shadows were signaling the end of the day. Then I walked to the house, which was about five minutes away. I was hungry. Mama didn't have a thing for me to eat. (This is one of the reasons why today I value food of any kind.) So I just lay down and went back to sleep.

The next morning, Mama gave me a piece of pork. She said I was to discard it because it was spoiling. It wasn't spoiling though; I smelled it, and I could tell that it would be okay to eat. Many years later I learned from her that it was her piece of pork and she had saved it for us kids.

*   *   *

The assault of our mama was preceded by the arrival of a soldier who didn't speak English. The group that followed had come from across the little river; that is how I knew the soldiers came from the Japanese military bodega farther up the river from our farm. The leader was probably a unit commander with his senior officer. They shouted at Mama, but of course she didn't understand. The leader shouted at her again and motioned for her to go upstairs, past the mounted monkey-eating eagle. The senior officer looked at us boys and assigned a soldier to each of us to take us away.

I was taken by one of the soldiers to an area behind the chicken nests. I contemplated running around him to get away, but I thought better of it and stood still. My assigned soldier could have shot or bayoneted me at any time. In the background I could see Bob climbing a pomelo tree while his soldier stood guard between him and the house. My guard started playing with the point of the bayonet, which was still affixed to his rifle, passing it around the navel of my protruding stomach. (I guess we all had a case of kwashiorkor.)

I was aware that during this time while he was drawing circles around my tummy, he could have run me through with his bayonet. Over many years since then, I have speculated on the story he would have told the officers; he would have gotten away with it.

I could see that Bob had climbed the tree and was watching activities on the second floor. I didn't have such a vantage point.

After the contingent of soldiers departed, I wanted to find out how Mama was doing. Bob told me that she didn't want to be bothered. I have learned since then that she was unconscious from having been struck on the jaw. Much later she was up and walking around with a washcloth. She didn't want to speak to any of her kids. Slowly she headed toward the water of Sunny Brook. I have never forgotten Mama's anguish when we kids tried to approach her and her pitifully swollen face, where she had evidently been struck very hard

Centipedes and Other Tropical Horrors

A lot of people call it a field mouse; but it is not. It is a vole. It was lying on its side, under a board that I had lifted. A long time ago, Mama had told us to not mess around with a dead animal, because it could have had diseases dangerous to humans. I turned the vole over and was almost snagged by the tail end of a foot-long reddish centipede. The difference is that both red and black centipedes are about the same length—about a foot in length—but the black ones are much more virulent than the red ones.

I recoiled in horror and then realized that the centipede was buried inside the vole. Something had neatly cut into the side of the vole—probably the jaws of the centipede. The vole's legs were shaking as though it were cold. It was a shivering motion. The vole appeared to be in a trance. The centipede's head was sucking at the vole's heart. It was drinking the blood of the vole.

I was angry, because the centipede, which was about one foot long, had invaded the innocent vole's body. I slammed the board down on top of it and jumped on the board. After a short while, I gingerly picked up the edge of the board. Right there in front of me was a smashed vole, his guts all over the place, and neatly disappearing down a hole was the centipede. I had miscalculated once more, and the centipede got away. What I had witnessed was a primary law of the jungle: food, no matter how it is obtained, is food! What I was angry at was probably an invasion of domain.

*   *   *

I could swear there were two types of poisonous snakes in the Philippines. The king cobra is one. I learned many, many years later that herpetologists have placed the Philippines in an area well-covered by the king cobra, which can grow as long as eighteen feet. Now that is a lot of poisonous snake! I have never seen a king cobra, although tenant farmers on our Sunny Brook Farm told me that they had seen one standing above them, looking down on them. (Rule of thumb: I learned that two-thirds of the snake must be on the ground in order to provide a foundation for the third standing above the ground.) My observation was that the second poisonous snake species was a *Naja naja*, which is a black snake with a yellowish or white belly. Those in the know have told me that these are adolescent king cobras. I disagree; I have seen many of the *Naja naja* species, but I have never knowingly seen a king cobra.

*   *   *

The people who know ants tell me that fire ants are red with a stinging bite. If my perceptions are correct, then we have fire ants all over the Philippines. Black ants, mostly found in vegetation, can bite like blazes too. There are many of these biting black ants in the Philippines, especially around the trunks of large trees; I know this from personal experience as a kid!

When I was about eight years old, I wanted to be a big man and emulate my father. He had such a soft heart that he would catch large black Mindanao wasps captured by our screen in the Tiongko Avenue house, where we lived after the war. He would catch them in a bathing towel, and I tried to do the same thing. I screamed because the wasp injected its venom into my hand through the towel.

*   *   *

Monkey-eating eagles are now extinct. Papa killed one of these enormous birds before the war, on one of his many jungle excursions. A taxidermist had done an excellent job. Its wings were folded against the body, and its claws were holding it onto a branch perch. The open wingspan would have been greater than twelve feet, according to Papa. In our Sunny Brook Farm, we placed the mounted bird at the entrance to the upstairs space that was our bedroom, where we met in a small circle every evening. We listened to our mama's tales about Mother Goose, and other wonderful stories. We kids believed that the big bird could protect us; we imagined that its fierce-looking visage would somehow save us from all forms of evil.

*   *   *

I had been told by the tenant farmers, their darkly spoken words verified by older brother Bob, that the wakwak tree was where evil spirits lived. The wakwak tree was an anomaly; it stood in splendid isolation surrounded by a field of tall clumps of cogon (a type of native grass). A well-worn path about 150 feet away from the tree had been created by thousands of feet, as the tenant farmers always bypassed the tree at a safe distance; no other paths went toward it from the main route. This was an indication to me that, over time, everyone had been avoiding the tree altogether.

Whenever the tenants talked about the tree, they crossed themselves (as all orthodox Catholics do when they beseech the Lord to protect them from any evil entity they may have inadvertently offended). A number of our farm laborers spoke about the wakwak tree in hushed tones, and then they seriously warned one another that it was to be shunned. No person that I knew ever went to it. But as usual, I was extremely curious, and I was young and didn't know any better, so one day, I hesitantly wended my way off the main path. I headed directly toward the mysterious tree, stealthily stepping through the cogon, which was much taller than me and was hiding my approach. Soon I was nearly to the edge of a large umbrella-like canopy of leafy branches extending from a rather modest-sized trunk.

I went no farther. In short order, I realized that what I could see under the giant tree were many bulbous, papery nests hanging down from the branches. Then I noticed the movement of hundreds of large Mindanao wasps going in and out of their domains. No longer curious and only wanting to get away from the wasps and whatever evil spirits they were protecting, I quickly returned to the main path. That was enough of the wakwak tree for me!

Delivering Food to American Teacher POWs

Early in the war and after we had taken our nighttime hike from our city home to the farm, Mama told Bob and me that we had to do a very important task: it would take all day long to accomplish it, but we just had to do it. Of course we would do it! We jumped at the chance of having another grand adventure—no matter that Bob was an estimated seven years old at the time and I only five.

Mama was anguished over the collecting of the American teachers into a concentration camp south of Talomo. She knew the area had no shade. It was hot. Her friends and compatriots, most of them fellow teachers, had been herded into a compound on a grassy hill overlooking the Davao Gulf, and they would probably not be provided food or water by the soldiers. So her priority at this time was to send food to her friends. She and Bob hooked a sled to one of our carabao (water buffalo—most of them were just mean, unruly beasts) and lashed a stock of bananas to the sled platform, and she sent us on a mission to take bananas to the prisoners. The responsibility was enormous. We were two children being sent out into an uncertain, hostile world to deliver food to needy people, and we weren't sure it would even get to the hands of those who needed it. We would need to walk about five miles toward the city and back again. After she repeated detailed instructions to Bob, she explained that she would have to stay because the babies were young and needed care.

Mama and Bob selected our most gentle carabao out of our small herd. On Mama's instructions, we went to one of our tenant farmers and hitched up to a travois-like sled that was already loaded with a stalk of bananas. A stalk of bananas is the prime fruit of a banana plant. Usually about eight to ten hands of bananas grow from the stalk, and approximately six to eight bananas may be found in each hand of bananas. One stalk of bananas was therefore very heavy; it was the maximum we could place on the sled.

"I want you to understand," she briefed us as we were ready to take off, "that American teachers like your father have been put in prison. They were put there just because they're American! Your guardian angel will be with you—she reassured us—and protect you the whole way. Now go!"

Starting out was not easy. Bob walked behind the sled as the carabao dragged it up the hill along the cogon-lined path. I dutifully walked up behind the entire parade, the cogon whipping my face. I was hot and sweaty, and I continually waved away hordes of flies—as did Bob, and as did the carabao with its flipping ears. It was a very hot day. The trip seemed unbearably long. It was uneventful, and I wanted to take a nap. "We have just started," my brother reminded me, but I wanted my nap anyhow. After several hours, during which I tried sleeping while walking but didn't succeed, we finally arrived at the rolled barbed wire fencing around the POW compound. "We're here," my brother eventually announced. "Don't say anything." Then he was gone. I stayed close to the carabao while Bob went searching for an entrance and someone to take our bananas.

Eventually Bob returned, and we proceeded with our stalk of bananas behind the carabao to the compound entrance. As we approached, I observed a very tall American wearing a pith helmet asking the Japanese soldier at the entrance, "Isn't there any drinking water available?" The guard did not speak English, so he simply gesticulated to show that he didn't know what the man was saying. (The guard, who was wearing a light-brown uniform and carrying a rifle with a bayonet, was playing dumb, because even as a five-year-old child I could see that the man needed a drink of water, as did all the women and children in the background, who were all prisoners also and who were probably members of his group.) I have wondered many times since then whether the tall, sunburned American ever got some water and if he even survived the war at all.

We had to leave our cargo with the Japanese guard, and I'm not sure the bananas ever got to the Americans. Nevertheless, my brother Bob repeated this excursion two more times, but without me. His departure was of no concern to me; what bothered me deeply was that plans had been made without my input. I complained, but Mama simply said that she didn't want to wake me from my afternoon nap. In the meantime, Bob continued with his long and lonely trips, and he returned much sooner on his own than he had with me. I never figured out the reason.

So many years later, I have had several opportunities to ask myself why Mama would risk our young lives to do such a thing. Even after lengthy analysis, the answer remains a mystery to me. Perhaps she was attempting to memorialize Papa, for she had often mentioned to all of us that she believed he had been captured by Japanese troops or was dead. Or maybe, on behalf of Filipino teachers, she was attempting to incur a favorable view of the Philippines among US teachers.

War Story Number Two

Our attorney in Davao City, Philippines, Raul O. Tolentino, has two war stories in this memoir. The following is the second one. This has to do with the partial destruction of the Bankerohan Bridge by his father, a member of US Army Forces in the Far East (USAFFE). Raul's father had orders to blow up the Bankerohan Bridge if an armed enemy unit approached the bridge. When the Japanese military force neared the bridge, the senior Tolentino went into action but was not able to complete his job because he had run out of explosives. He had not been provided sufficient dynamite or other explosives to successfully finish the job as directed. He just used what he had available and left the bridge in disrepair but not completely taken down.

Had he been able to do the job as instructed, our desperate contingent of Mama and four kids with a little red wagon never would have been able to escape the city and go to the farm. We would have turned around, gone back to the home we had evacuated, and probably starved to death—and this book would not have been published more than seventy years later.

Warplanes, Navy Ships, and Shrapnel

The first few times a brown Piper Cub with a big white star on its side showed up, we ran out and waved at it. Mama joined us the first time. Soon after, we saw the plane fly beyond the hills, and each time it did so, shelling would begin. Mama then told us not to wave at the planes. She said, "The Japanese will see us as friends of the planes, and that would not be a good thing."

In addition to the airplanes, we experienced shelling by US Navy ships several miles away, out in the Davao Gulf. There were many explosions, all above the ground, in the air. Once I looked up right at an explosion. It was white, and there was a blossoming of heat, along with many small metallic pieces that ripped through the banana leaves. This was exciting stuff until Mama screamed at me to get away. I learned later that those ripping sounds were made by shrapnel that came from shells designed to explode high in the air in order to rain destructive metal shards on targets below.

After every shelling, Bob and I would go around to collect pieces of sharp metal from the fields. We filled oval sardine cans. And he told me we had to collect the pieces quickly, as otherwise they would rust and discolor in the heat and humidity and become indistinguishable from the soil. Whenever shells whizzed and scissored through the nipa hut and leaves of nearby banana and abaca plants, we knew that nearby we could look for metal shards.

Then, like other boys collecting marbles, the challenge was to determine whose shrapnel was the best. Bob always claimed to be the winner of these contests; his had the best blue color, were the shiniest, sharpest, longest—whatever! That was all right with me; he was the oldest, after all. But I did keep searching.

At the time, I didn't really pay much attention to where our shrapnel originated. In later years I learned that most US Navy ships could lob rounds for distances of twenty-five miles. Further recent research turned up the fact that the vessel that was shelling us from the Gulf of Davao during WWII was the USS *Denver*—named in honor of the very same city I would eventually call home, and where now, in 2015, I am writing my memoirs.

* * *

I heard the engines first: four times three airplanes—that's twelve loud engines! They were B17 Flying Fortress bombers, probably on a reconnaissance mission for the enemy forces in Davao Gulf. I heard them, but they were obscured by the pomelo fruit trees and flying to the south of us.

Twelve engines make quite a racket. Mama and Bob came rushing out of the house, followed by toddler Becky. The planes were slightly banking and flying toward Mintal and were not dropping bombs. I heard Mama shout: "Higher, higher. Oh, they are too low!"—as if the pilots could hear her. She was wishing they could destroy the Japanese military installation across the river from us. The bombers, amid a cloud of exploding antiaircraft shells, kept on flying toward the little town, farther into the interior.

There was a lead bomber, and the others flew in a trail behind it. The last one, trying hard to keep up with the other two, had been hit by antiaircraft fire and lost the right wing; that side was toward us. The left wing continued to give lift to the whole airplane, and the fuselage rotated toward us. The whole bomber then lost altitude, and we did not see any parachutes come out of the airplane.

I understand that there were a couple of parachutes seen by the populace of the city. The crewmembers who had been able to open their parachutes landed in the fire of the crashed airplane, however. Many days later, the local newspaper carried a photograph of a young aircrew member, and he was alive, but not for long. Standing right behind the kneeling prisoner was a Japanese soldier (presumably an officer) raising a katana. He was about to decapitate the kneeling airman. The helpless young man had his hands tied behind his back. For many years I had childhood nightmares visualizing a sword cutting through a person's neck.

As the remaining two bombers flew over Mintal, a Japanese fighter plane was able to fly directly at the tail gunner of the second aircraft. A .50-caliber shell must have gotten him right through the chest, because the plane went straight down, without any fire or smoke. I mentioned this to my brother Bob, who just shrugged. After all, he had seen enough!

For the longest time, we all stood riveted in a tight group, watching a B-17 falling to the ground in flames. Then, for some reason, Mama moved forward a step or two—much as if an unseen force contemplated short term results (plenty of blood and a dead Mama) and long-term results (four immediately created orphans who would never make it without her guidance and daily efforts). I wanted to follow Mama, since she was my source of comfort in stressful times like this, but my feet would not move.

Suddenly an AA shell about the size of a tennis ball came sizzling into the spot between us where Mama had been standing moments before. (It had her name on it, as we say in current times.) The shell easily embedded itself into the ground, which was especially hard as the result of a long period of drought.

Mama looked back at us in horror, and I realized later as an adult that at that moment she became a confirmed believer in her own God. She warned us away from the hole, knowing that the shell could still explode at any time. A few days later, a tenant farmer came by, and Mama instructed him to carefully dig out the AA shell. He informed us that it was buried at least two feet deep and evidently it was a dud. Nonetheless, it was a traumatic experience for us that I will never forget.

Many, many years later, I read in one of Mama's many books that the Greek gods used to play games with humans because humans could do some independent thinking. On this day when a shell almost hit Mama, it seemed these gods were playing games with our little Sunny Brook family. We were the only people for miles around and yet seemed to be specially targeted by a lone, random antiaircraft (AA) shell.

* * *

Early one morning, Bob suddenly left the farm alone, heading for Libby Airfield, which was being used by the planes we often saw flying overhead. Even though he could have been captured, tortured, and then shot, I was simply angry because he didn't take me along—how naive I was!

On his return, he had an exciting report for me about watching a P38 Lightning strafe the field. Each time the pilot reached the end, he would do a cuban eight (also called a lazy eight) and come by again, strafing the other direction. He explained that a P38 was a twin-fuselage fighter airplane and that it was very effective because it did not require a synchronization mechanism for the bullets from the machine gun it carried to fire through its own propeller. In other words, its propellers were located at the end of each fuselage. I wished I could have seen that display myself (I, who had no more sense than to stand upright when a soldier urinated in the nearby field). At this stage of the game, Japanese soldier patrols were looking for infiltrators, such as my brother, and would have fired at any movement that they detected. It is no wonder he wanted to go alone.

*   *   *

There was only one bomber overhead. It was a B-25 Mitchell medium bomber, and Mama, as usual, hoped it would find the Japanese military bodega across the river to be a target of opportunity. She swore at the Japanese soldiers across the river: "Get the SOBs! Get the lummoxes! Get 'em, get 'em." My brother Bob climbed a pomelo tree to see what was causing damage to a tree across the creek. It was a shell from the bomber. The shell did not explode in the bodega as Mama had hoped; it caved the roof in, however.

Increasing Terror and Desperation

After evacuating our city home to live at Sunny Brook Farm, our only source of medicines was a medical doctor who lived on a distant part of the farm with his beautiful family of kids our age and a young-looking, pretty wife. For some reason, we Oliver kids had an innate mistrust of him. Once I watched him create powder from what looked like an aspirin tablet then dilute the powder with pure, clean (so Mama later told me) water from a clear glass bottle. Then he sucked the liquid from a teaspoon with a hypodermic needle and administered injections to everybody except Bob.

I don't know when Bob disappeared or where he disappeared to, but it seemed to me that if his brothers and little sister were expected to experience pain from an inoculating needle, then Bob should be subjected to the same treatment. I remember voicing my opinion to Mama, but she dismissed the pesky child at her elbow with the wave of a hand. It just seemed to me that my elder brother Bob had special privileges. As a young child, I had no problem with use of the needle. After all, I had watched as Mama also was inoculated with the same needle, and everything seemed just fine with me. (At the time, I was a only a four-year-old kid who had no idea what sterilization of hypodermic needles entailed.)

The doctor and his family lived in a well-furnished, well-kept, and well-appointed home. They were like our family in a number of ways; I think Mama simply liked to converse with the doctor and members of his family because they were formally educated and could carry on a long and meaningful conversation, unlike many of our compatriots, who could not. I don't know what arrangements he had made with Mama, but as a professional, he probably bartered an exchange of daily living space for his family in exchange for medicine as needed and periodic medical checkups on us kids.

At this time, Davao City and its proximity was being heavily reinforced by the Japanese high command, who had expected the Allied liberation invasion in that area. We children were American mestizos; we were light-skinned because of our papa, and neighbors seldom came by to visit Mama. They feared retaliation of some sort since the Japanese were always on the prowl for what they considered subversive activity.

As children we could detect heavy uncertainty and dread as Mama occasionally talked with tenants or neighbors who infrequently came by. They all agreed that Japanese activity was on the increase, but no one knew why. Patrols were more frequent through the farm and surrounding area, and rumors were widespread of an increase in the brutal nature of the soldiers.

Mama had also heard that people were again being ordered to evacuate their homes, and the edict was a strong one: those who refused would be shot. But we had already left our homes in the city, and she was not sure where we were to go if we left the farm. There seemed to be enough urgency that we had to move very soon. Besides, food was once again becoming very scarce, and time was running out for those who had no place to go.

Finally, one night Mama told Bob to go the doctor's home and ask him what he knew about the martial orders. Perhaps he could also obtain some guidance about what to do next. Mama's orders to us: "Jim will go along. Take care of him. Jim, you take care of Bob, and you listen to what he tells you to do. Both of you must be very careful. Your guardian angel will watch over you. Now, go!"

I was not frightened as we set off in the dark. I was simply going off on an assignment with my older brother, upon whose shoulders I could literally stand whenever danger appeared that night; I had asked, and he had told me so. Over the passing of years, I've had a chance to imagine how terrified I would have been if he had been removed from the scene.

In the heavy black of night, we started out from the farmhouse, moving along a path lined with grass and vines. I was very afraid of things out there in the dark, and I dutifully strode close behind my brother in the night—so near to him that his brushings against cogon blades were also my own. More than once I ran into him in the blackness of the night, as he would stop suddenly in order to intently listen to what was ahead in the darkness. Then he would get angry at me for automatically forging ahead and not helping him listen for dangers in front of us.

Well, what was I supposed to do? Everything he told me was ingested into this huge cavity called my head, which is where brains supposedly reside—and any detailed information Bob told me just disappeared and became invisible! I tried to relate it to something that I knew, as then it would make sense to me, but I could not relate this experience to anything familiar. I was simply too young to meet my elder brother's sensible expectations.

He even took the time to tell me what we should both be listening for—Japanese troops setting up a night ambush; a call of some night bird, which was a sure sign of a snake nearby; or somebody on the path ahead of us—and I nodded as if he could see in the blackness of the night that I fully understood exactly what he had just told me.

We would start out once more, and within five minutes of hiking, I would run into him again in the darkness. A fat lot of good his lecturing me turned out—for both of us. Everywhere was pitch-black, but Bob quietly led us along the path through the cogon. Out there in the dark we occasionally heard noises from outposts where Japanese soldiers stealthily moved. I kept thinking that these groups of adults were a source of comfort and security and that if something went terribly wrong (and I was abandoned for some reason by my brother Bob), I would head to one of these Japanese outposts. I was terribly naive then; walking in by myself would have been a blatant and immediate invitation to be bayoneted. An introspective analysis of my situation many years later shows that simply being bayoneted would have been the very least of my worries.

When we approached the doctor's house, we both were aware of the terror in the crying voices of his wife and children and other relatives. Apparently the afternoon had been spent by the family celebrating some relative's birthday—or perhaps it was the old man's birthday, or something else that required the presence of relatives. In any event, there were a bunch of relatives there. The furniture stood where the wall should have started, and since the wife was such a model housekeeper, the breezes flowed through the open patio room as if they graced her and had been designed for a close, festive occasion. Everything was picture-perfect. Then along came the Japanese soldiers, led by their commander, marching in troop formation through the head-high cogon, which hid them for the longest time as murder and bullying played in their eyes.

The leader of the group of soldiers was shouting out orders, and the farm people were screaming as they were bullied. Somebody had already been bayoneted in the house, and I thought it was the doctor. Just then a Japanese soldier dragged a body by one arm out of the main nipa hut and onto the *sala*, a living room arranged so that the room had only a thatched roof but no walls. A lamp sputtered on one of the corner posts, and I realized that though it had a lot of good coconut oil in it, water had somehow been mixed in its fuel, causing it to sputter. I also thought that in any other circumstance, the arrangement would have been a pleasant place in which to take a nap in an easy chair during an afternoon thunderstorm.

Bob told me to hide and led us to crouch behind a large tomato plant beside the path a short way from the house. The Japanese soldiers' shouting and bullying continued. Finally the shouted orders ceased and quiet despair prevailed. The soldiers collected in a group and then marched by us in single file, their boots tramping along the path next to our tomato plant. We crouched lower but were so close we could have reached out and touched them as they filed by.

It was a black, moonless night, so when I looked up, I saw a clear sky with faraway pinpoints of stars. Some of the stars were very bright, but they also seemed very alone, even though there were many of them.

In the blackness, we were just able to make out that someone was leading away the very sad eldest boy—maybe a son still grieving for a recently bayoneted father. He had a very dark and heavy wet smear across most of his face, and his arms were tied behind his back. Somehow I just knew I would never see him again, because—heavy wet smear across his face or not—the Japanese soldiers were not done with him. Even at my young age, I could predict that his Mama would never look upon him again.

Nevertheless, someone had been alive just a few minutes before; now he was dead and there was blood all over the floor of the nipa hut. The blood looked like a pool of engine oil, except the pool kept getting larger and larger until a surrealism of sorts took over. Somehow I just knew the human body didn't carry that much liquid.

A Japanese soldier suddenly turned and looked directly at me (or so I thought), and I became embarrassed. I stood up, saying to myself, "Okay, you got me! You saw me even though I thought I was well hidden. But now you see me." It was a dangerous game I was playing. Bob looked in my direction and saw me standing. "Get down!" he commanded. I looked at him; he was angry. I got down. I was angry at my brother for being angry with me. I recall looking down in the darkness, and I simply started to mess around in the sandy soil with a stick I had located. The soldier came right up to us. In two more very short steps, he could easily have stepped on us. But then he stopped.

There were some rustling sounds, and then, in front of us, he began urinating. By just standing and shouting, I could have terribly frightened him. (It has occurred several times to me that we could also have been terribly dead had he or anyone else in the group detected us.) Had he turned about forty-five degrees to his right, he could easily have urinated on me! The tomato plants moved about, and then he was gone. He had rejoined his unholy group at the nipa hut, where the officer was still shouting at the sobbing woman who was distressed that her husband was still lying at everyone's feet in the pool of blood. He had not moved an inch. Today I would assess that someone in such a state was already dead. If we had arrived a few minutes earlier, Bob and I probably would have been part of the surprised group. We would have had a lot of explaining to do about why we were there and why we weren't relatives like the other people. Eventually we would have been forced to lead the entire contingent of Kempeitai troops back to Mama and our Sunny Brook home.

I remember that the soldier's eyes were glazed and reflected the solitary flame of the coconut oil lamp, which caused shadows to dance about. He was the one who probably had thrust the bayonet into the doctor's gut. (Many years later I learned from various readings that a bayonet thrust to the gut area of a victim would be a painful way to die, because it would take hours to die from pierced intestines. The pain could be frightful.) The flickering flames from the sputtering single lantern that hung over the doctor's carcass cast shadows outward, creating a scene in which the shadows were prominent although they flickered. That is likely the reason the soldier didn't see two tiny boys crouched among the tomato plants: the shadows morbidly, fearsomely, had been dancing all about.

As the night wore on, I reacquired my playful mood of great adventure, and Bob and I used the dancing shadows as camouflage by stealthily moving only when night breezes caused shadows to appear most plentiful in our area. We crouched as low as we could, stole past the tomato plants, and finally were on our way home. We still had miles to go in the pitch-black darkness, and we still had to hike past the wakwak tree. That was the part that I didn't look forward to. It was the wakwak's night. She was getting even for some offense we had done her in the recent past. (Why the offense had to be recent, I don't know, but it seemed an important matter to me at the time.)

I don't remember many details of our outbound and return trips, but after a long time we finally arrived home. I do remember coming back to a pitch-black home, a sure sign to me that something was terribly wrong. But everything was fine, after all. It was simply Mama's way of implementing a security measure. She had stayed awake the entire time we had been gone. Bob explained what had taken place: the death of the doctor and the misery of the family. After hearing our dismal report, Mama felt she was completely out of options to protect her family.

Mama became instantly agitated when she heard about the bayonetting of our doctor and our description of the widening pool of his blood. She just didn't know what to do. Her perplexity was apparent. It showed in the aimless walks she took around our rudimentary kitchen. It was also evident after a long, long time, perhaps hours on end, she spent suddenly waving her hands and arms at no one in particular. I recollect falling asleep after our report and wanting to sleep forever.

Much later, as I became many years older, I've thought of this event several times. Usually I have concluded that I was just too young and perhaps just too stupid to understand that the entire situation was fraught with danger. I didn't have a sense of purpose; nor did I have an idea of what a mission was. Yet my older brother, Bob, possessed both traits. I was unwilling to concede that because he was a couple of years older than I, he was wiser than I was—even if by only two years.

* * *

The next morning, after Bob and I had stealthily walked through the blackness of that fateful night to the doctor's home and back, the whole family had picked up on Mama's frantic concern. We were all wary and incessantly anticipating a patrol of Japanese soldiers with murder in their eyes. Then, through divine intervention—according to Mama—Eddie and Manolo showed up. Mama later told us that their appearance was like a message from heaven, as we had a much better chance of surviving with them in the picture. I think that once again she was given reason to believe—really believe—in the existence of God. At least she had an answer to the many queries with which she had been burdened from her inquisitive kids. When they unexpectedly showed up at the farm, the entire picture of our existence suddenly changed for Mama.

Eddie and Manolo were both strapping, energetic young boys of about twelve, I would guess. For some reason they sought us out at Sunny Brook. I had the impression they truly admired Papa, the *Americano* teacher and guerilla leader. I don't believe they were associated with any anti-Japanese movement or group. They were just dynamic, energetic, and especially full of the need to help their school supervisor and superintendent where they could. Also, I think they became involved when Mama dropped a hint to somebody that we needed help.

Possibly Eddie and Manolo were more driven by curiosity than anything else. As a youngster who should have known there existed a host of possibilities, I never questioned my mama as to why the two were the same age and described each other as brothers yet didn't look alike. They were just very good friends. I do remember quite clearly that Eddie was talkative, perhaps a bit effusive, while Manolo tended to be quiet and almost shy. I also remember that Eddie was the planner, and Manolo just followed him and did whatever Eddie had said both of them should do.

Apparently, as every local war refugee did, Eddie and Manolo must have unobtrusively walked past Japanese military outposts and then hiked several miles to just show up at the farm. In those years, I had concluded that everybody knew the location of Catalunan Pequeño. Since the location of Catalunan Grande, on the other side of our Sunny Brook, was well known to the general public, I reasoned, at five years of age, that everyone should therefore know where Catalunan Pequeño would be—and that was where the Olivers lived. Logic at the age of five just makes so much sense.

Mama told Eddie and Manolo her story of desperation with no hope for a solution. I was full of five-year-old wisdom but didn't have anything to add to the conversation. I had sense enough, however, to keep quiet. Mama had heard rumors from passing tenants and farmers that refugees were being killed by the thousands—"butchered," Mama sagely interpreted—by Japanese soldiers at Talomo, especially at the juncture of the Mintal and Talomo roads. (That is exactly the route Bob and I, two small American mestizo kids, had taken just a few months before with our load of bananas and the gentle carabao pulling our sled.)

Immediate Departure for Kawá-Kawá

In graphic detail, Mama passed her considerable concerns for our safety on to Eddie and Manolo. They knew that after combining what she told them with what they had learned from others, we all had to abandon the area immediately. According to hastily made plans, we would leave our home again that very night. The destination, both young boys suggested in hushed tones, was Kawá-Kawá—an area known as the Devil's Cauldron. There was complete agreement on the mysterious destination toward the interior, as well as the compressed and urgent schedule for an imminent departure. The brothers assured Mama they would be able to lead us there. She had to consider the options available to her family for less than a moment before agreeing with the recommendations of her former students.

Both boys then disappeared. They were simply gone, perhaps to get some rest. (I thought they would have to get some sleep, as they faced a long night ahead of them.) After all, by assuming the personal safety of an entire family of mostly kids just when evening shadows were growing long, Eddie and Manolo, actually just young boys themselves, had adopted an extreme load of responsibilities—likely far beyond what they ever before encountered. I assume they went back home to the city to describe their intentions and plans to parents who had told them to be careful.

Mama then got her kids together and told us that we had to play together close to home and keep quiet the whole day long. None of what she directed was going to be easy for a seven-year-old (my brother, Bob), a five-year-old (me), and a three-year-old who simply refused to be bullied by two older brothers (Becky). Winston, still a tiny baby, was asleep and wouldn't be that much involved in complying with Mama's orders. It seemed to me that he slept all the time.

Years later, in answer to our questions about Eddie and Manolo, Mama told us they were just school kids who were her students, and they were simply being loyal to their teacher. She also told all of us that Eddie and Manolo were several years too young to have been involved in the resistance movement. Guerillas, as everyone knew, were all warriors whose intentions were always to kill Japanese soldiers. She also explained to us that members of the formal resistance ranged all the way from active guerilla fighters to plain old haulers of supplies and foodstuffs. Initially the haulers had a rough go of it. When they were stopped and searched by the invading troops, they had to provide detailed reasons for making their shipments, including the use of every item they were carrying. If they were not able to provide reasons that the soldiers found acceptable, they were tortured to death on the spot.

*   *   *

Mama put together our survival kit—a precious hodgepodge of a few clothes; a couple of pans, packed so they would not make noise; and a cup. There were barely enough pieces to sustain anyone—only so many that if we were surprised by soldiers on the way, we wouldn't seem like a fleeing family following an organized plan. Also, there was nothing burdensome or heavy enough to fatigue us or slow us down.

As darkness came, we peered into the blackness. When Mama called out in a whisper, Eddie suddenly materialized and found us huddled together. Manolo disappeared to be a lookout. Eddie said they hadn't been able to find us in the dark and had been about to leave but decided to look once more. Mama told him she heard noises but didn't know it was them.

Just as we left the farm to start upriver, Bob said he heard cogon grass swishing against Japanese soldiers' uniforms. A patrol had been sent out, and each member of the patrol had murder in his eyes, I'm sure. This was the patrol that had been sent for us. All day long, we had waited for them, and Mama had intended to talk nicely to them, but even as a child I thought differently. I knew they had been sent to kill us. It turned out that we had departed only a few seconds before they arrived. They found an empty farmhouse.

We headed up Sunny Brook in the dark, crossing and recrossing it several times, stopping once in a while as Eddie and Manolo went ahead. The brook got larger, and after a while there was the constant roaring of a large river next to us. There were shushes to keep quiet and not make noise. We scurried, stooped over, always taking cover and then stumbling on through the dark. Becky cried once but was hushed into quietness. The darkness was full of mosquitoes. It seemed as if we walked forever in the dark of night.

After a long, exhausting night of constant walking in the dark next to a roaring river, morning arrived. We emerged into a dry, very hot clearing in a valley. The earth was covered with red clumps, probably clay. The cogon grass was sparse. There were a few abaca plants a short distance away, and there a settlement of refugees had formed; there were rudimentary nipa huts and nothing but bare ground in between them. Within a stone's throw from the huts was a Japanese outpost. Bob was sent to look the situation over. The civilian people were unwelcoming, and the Japanese soldiers were mean looking. Mama had already decided she wouldn't settle in the small community. We would stay where we were, away from the others.

Eddie and his friend returned in the morning to put up a nipa hut for us. They arrived with bamboo, flats of cut grass, and several palm tree fans. They dug postholes, tightly lashed some crosspieces, and then departed. They came back later, did some work, and then departed once more—only to return hours later to work again. Later, I got the drift through hushed conversation that they didn't want to raise any suspicion from the Japanese outpost that we were a cohesive unit. Eddie and Manolo didn't want any attention at all.

As they methodically, bit by bit, built our nipa hut, they also dug a trench below our hut. It was a short trench we could all roll into when shelling began or at the onset of any other dangers Mama might perceive and tell us about.

*　　*　　*

Soon after our arrival in Kawá-Kawá, we saw a small, pudgy man with squinty angry-looking eyes approaching us through the line of abaca, crossing the field from the main settlement to where we stood. He presented himself as though he were the king of Kawá-Kawá. Mama fielded his nosy questions and then verbally indicated we had nothing more to say to him, and with an obvious smirk on his face, the man departed. I call him the Judas Man, as I can't recall his real name. Mama conveyed to us that he was a Japanese collaborator, mostly to assuage our curiosity and incessant questions. She emphasized he was a treacherous man.

This obnoxious Judas Man returned time and again, asking the same questions: Where were we from? Who was our father? Where was he now? Mama disliked him immediately and told us not to talk with him, but he would go away with a smirk then return later to ask more prying questions. Mama once told Bob to follow him. The Judas Man went straight to the Japanese outpost to talk with some of the soldiers and their translators.

*　　*　　*

Mama had brought an aluminum pan and a cup in our evacuation belongings. Our meals weren't many. We would have an occasional soup, mostly from a single potato-like *gábi*. Eddie and Manolo once brought an *ibid* (spiny-backed lizard) tied to a stick they carried between them. Mama recoiled, and they merrily laughed. They returned later with chunks of roasted, but very bony, lizard meat. Bob located water, which was scarce, so mama could cook something, but there was nothing to cook. We would hang around, waiting for something to eat. Mama would tell us, "Go out and play. Do something." She suffered more than her own hunger pangs; her heart ached that her children were slowly starving and she could do nothing about it. My brother Bob and I would occasionally come across a cassava plant (known as kamoteng kahoy in the local Visayan language).

This is a tropical plant with thick roots and a dark purplish skin used to make tapioca. We called it a wood potato, and after it was boiled it tasted a little bit like a potato. Once in a while, we could find a *camote* plant, which was a sweet potato or yam-like root crop. I also learned that if you are hungry long, your appetite disappears.

*   *   *

After all they did for our little struggling family, Eddie and Manolo lost their lives, and never returned to their homes and families in Davao City. The Judas Man of the Kawá-Kawá settlement accused Eddie and shy Manolo of evil deeds against elements of Japanese military forces. The mere accusation was enough for sadistic soldiers (whom I strongly believe were of the Kempeitai bunch) to torture the young students to death. Their torturers didn't really want any information at all; they just wanted to hear their fellow human beings scream and beg for mercy. I am convinced that Eddie and Manolo were tortured to death amid laughing soldiers of the Kempeitai.

The Japanese soldiers responsible for their deaths could not have cared less if the parents of the boys knew where their graves were. I myself don't precisely know where Eddie and Manolo are buried, but I know they were dead, because after several days, we began smelling their bodies; the smell emanated from the bamboo grove where they had been taken for their torture. I will always remember the smell of a decaying body. Decaying flesh smells just like a ripe ham, believe it or not.

Besides, during that time, while I was around seven years old, I had also seen the tight-lipped, sweaty, pale grave digger walk past our nipa hut, escorted by a rifle-bearing Japanese soldier who was simply doing the duty he had been assigned. A short while later, I saw both of them walking back to Kawá-Kawá village. The grave digger looked relieved that he hadn't simply been shot after his work was done. The soldier also looked relieved that he hadn't had to work and sweat in the hot sun to dig an extra grave for the grave digger as well. It was evident to me that grave digging to accommodate the bodies was finished for the day.

*   *   *

The Kempeitai was a feared organization, the Japanese military equivalent in the Pacific of the German military Gestapo in the European theater. The Kempeitai was historically responsible for the majority of atrocities in the Pacific theater during WWII. The most heinous of atrocities committed can be traced to this organization. Suffice it to state that this was just a plain nasty bunch. They tortured for the fun of it. They tortured adults not for information but to hear them cry out loud. Being a member of the Kempeitai was not an admirable existence.

In later years, we asked Mama about the Kempeitai, or Japanese military police. She verified that it was a feared organization and that it would not do anyone any good to become tangled up with that group. There were many people dead because they had tried to befriend the Kempeitai. Also, Davao Province had been assigned a much greater percentage of Kempeitai soldiers during the occupation than had been assigned to other regions of the Philippines. I was able to verify this much later, during research for this book.

*   *   *

On one very hot afternoon, we kids were some distance from our ragged nipa hut. I heard a disturbance, and when I looked up through the cogon, I saw Mama being grabbed by the arm and pulled toward the settlement by two Japanese soldiers. They were accompanied by the translator and the Judas Man. She was shouting hoarsely because they were trying to take her away without knowledge of any of us kids. I ran through the long blades of grass to her. Bob materialized from somewhere, and Becky showed up too. We didn't know what was going on or what we were supposed to do. Winston, as always, was close to her. The baby was frail and was kept in the shade.

When we three kids showed up, the soldiers released Mama. I believe they saw some futility in this situation, as well as that an exacerbation of the situation could lead to four orphans being let loose in Kawá-Kawá. The Judas Man continued exhorting them, however. The group finally turned away with their translator, while the small, pudgy evil man continued after them, gesticulating, shouting, and pleading. Mama told us to never again stray far from the hut and to stay close by always.

*   *   *

One morning we realized everyone had left the Kawá-Kawá Devil's Cauldron area without telling us! Mama was at the end of her tolerance, and on that day, I believe that she had run out of hope as well, because there were absolutely no inhabitants left in the nearby village. Also, there wasn't any movement near the Japanese military compound. Bob volunteered to go in closer to check the village for inhabitants, but Mama forbade it. I think she had a premonition that something was terribly, ominously wrong about the cluster of homes to the north of our nipa hut; it was just too silent in that direction.

I surmise that all one thousand or so of the village inhabitants were awakened from their sound sleep at bayonet point by the Japanese soldiers, who shushed the would-be victims with a finger to the lips, the universal signal for silence. Then the occupants of the entire village were marched toward the main concentration of Japanese soldiers near Mintal. At that location, I believe, they were systematically killed.

On some future day, a local farmer will plow his fields and a human femur will show up. He will stop his work to contact local authorities, and they will then send out a couple of experts, who will then dig up some more human bones. A mass grave will have been uncovered, and there among the bones and artifacts will be a clue that will lead more experts to the original site of the Devil's Cauldron, a village that we lived close to for a while—a village called Kawá-Kawá. And soon enough, no person now living will know there was even such a place on the face of this earth.

Realizing we were all alone with unknown danger that could show up at any moment, Mama struck out on her own. Without a word, in a state of near hysteria, she simply went in the opposite direction. Perhaps she was guided by the imposing Mount Apo, which always helped me with directions; it was to my right as we started heading downhill. We were practically running away from the Devil's Cauldron and toward Sunny Brook Farm.

We kids picked up on her terror and followed closely behind as best we could, without further comment or questioning. The area we were passing through was all contested land, and neither the Japanese or American field commanders could tell anyone, not even their own personnel, who was in control of it. After walking nonstop all day, we finally arrived at Sunny Brook Farm. I mostly remember the nipa hut, so we probably stopped there for the night.

The next day, Mama quietly scouted out the farmhouse to be sure it was not occupied by Japanese troops, while Bob was left in charge of the kids. We all remained alert for any signs of a Japanese patrol. When Mama determined it was safe, we were then permitted access to the farmhouse. The ever-present mosquitoes continued to eat us alive.

Later in the day, Mama and Bob had gone through the cogon to reach a second entrance to Sunny Brook. They were getting water for the family use. This access was up the hill in front of the house and down a steep embankment. Bob later told me that on the other side of the stream he saw a small group in US Army uniforms—not the expected Japanese. The soldiers signaled silently with fingers in front of their mouths, and Mama and Bob recognized the instructions to be quiet and not tell anyone. None of us knew what happened to the US Army unit after that encounter. We didn't know where they came from, and we certainly didn't know where they were headed. Without any actual verbal communication, they just disappeared. Bob and Mama returned to the farmhouse with water for us.

Only years later did I figure out that this was a surprise meeting with a US Army LRRP. I also learned that the acronym is pronounced as "lurp" and stands for "long-range reconnaissance patrol." Being a member of a long-range reconnaissance patrol (LRRP) is extremely dangerous, because members of the group are unprotected by a unit that the enemy can identify. Since an LRRP carries no identification insignia, the enemy commander wouldn't know the unit or anything else. Every member of an LRRP is fair game for immediate torture and execution, compared to a soldier in uniform with identifying information and possible protection by Geneva Convention wartime rules.

*   *   *

On arriving at the farm nipa hut after our sudden departure from the region known as the Devil's Cauldron, Mama learned, after four years, that our father was alive. She recognized his handwriting in a chalk-scrawled message that had been written on the lid of the old US Army trunk we had been using in our "plan B" nipa hut for storage. The message essentially said, "I was here; I don't know where you and the kids are. I will return."

How he got as far into the interior as he evidently did is still a mystery to me, because the entire countryside was still contested country, meaning that one couldn't tell on a map whether American or Japanese troops controlled the area.

There was more to the message, but I was as ignorant then, as much as I am today, regarding what a man and his wife say to each other upon meeting when there has been no communication between them for more than four years. I recall there was later civil discussion between them several times, but the word "hostage" would surface, and then the discussion would somehow end.

I believe Mama was in shock because she had thought that Papa had been dead for a matter of years, yet she had recognized his handwriting and the way he phrased the message.

The Dangerous Rescue

Papa carried a tommy gun. He was armed to the teeth and traveled with two Filipino trail scouts who were also well armed. Each of the scouts carried a bolo as well. (A bolo is a pointed, sharp knife. I have one that the Filipino contingent presented me in 1971 while I was province psychological warfare advisor during the Vietnam War.)

We kids and Mama were at our family nipa hut early afternoon one day when the rescuing trio showed up. The Filipino scouts were scary; their eyes were frightening to look at. They were ready to meet Japanese soldiers at any time and run them through with the bolos. In my mind, these two were dangerous, but at least I knew they were on our side. They said few words to us, and fewer words to each other, as they guarded our path in the cogon, with one of them in front of our family group and one in back.

Papa was talking to Mama, and I did not even recognize him as my dad. He told Mama, "We can't stay here very long; round up the kids and start moving." He then called to his scouts to come in, and we all obeyed his orders. As a group, we moved toward the highway, which was about three miles away. This was contested country, and our papa had inside information that we would not be safe there any longer.

When we got to the highway, Papa was able to hail a passing American military convoy; they recognized his uniform and rank as a US Army major. To make room for our family, a shirtless GI with a tommy gun moved to ride on the hood of the truck. As we drove away, Becky was crying, and we all turned to see our faithful dog Tanny trying to run fast enough to keep up with us. The dog could not come with us. The last I saw of our friend Tanny, he was disappearing in the dust far behind the truck.

Understanding that losing Tanny was difficult for all of us, he gave us each a candy bar. I took one bite of mine, wrapped it up, and put it in my pocket. Such a treasure needed to be saved and eaten bit by bit, not all at once! Several days later, I realized the precious candy bar was still in my pocket. Upon opening the wrapper, I saw a moldy, melted mess and had to throw it away after all.

The rescuing convoy took us about five miles to the US naval depot at Talomo Beach. We must have eaten upon our arrival. I don't remember what we slept on, but this was the first time in a very long time that any of us had slept and someone else was doing the guarding. Around three in the morning, we heard the report of a rifle shot; in kid fashion, I surmised the target was Tanny.

We remained at Talomo for several days, and evidently arrangements were made for our return to Davao City. We did not return to our Mapa Street home, where we had lived before the war, but took up residence in another of our mama's family homes about two blocks away, on Tiongko Arellano.

*   *   *

Over the years, my siblings and I have suffered from influences of our numerous childhood diseases. There were many. None of us had our childhood vaccinations, including the one for diphtheria, pertussis, and typhoid (DPT). In addition, we were vulnerable to diarrhea, dysentery, and, of course, malaria. I have experienced malaria chills on two separate occasions—once as a nineteen-year-old during work on the Erie Railroad, and again as a major during the Vietnam War. Years and years later, I was shown US Air Force X-rays taken of my lungs, showing that I have tubercular scars from childhood exposure to TB.

Cholera, dysentery, TB, diphtheria, tetanus, pertussis, malaria—none of us Oliver kids had access to medical treatments, so we simply toughed it out when we caught diseases. During this period of vulnerability as a child is probably when I was exposed to hepatitis C. A physician at Denver General Hospital told me in 1998 (just before my wife and I traveled to Hong Kong and the interior of China) that I caught hepatitis somewhere and that I now had a natural immunity to it.

*   *   *

The following story was related to me by a young man named Adriano, who helped around our home in Davao City after the war as a handyman and a houseboy.

When the tables were turned so Filipino guerillas were hunting Japanese soldiers, a soldier had been captured by the guerillas. They had unceremoniously dropped him off at a common community gathering location for Davao City's population. His hands were tied behind his back with rattan strips, and his mouth was soon bulging with bodies of dead rats that the people had stuffed in. Then the Japanese soldier was buried alive. A few people sharpened rattan strips and pierced his lips with the bamboo-like skewers after tails and bodies of dead rats had been shoved into his mouth. His eyes showed fear and just plain despair as the men shoveled dirt, mostly sand, on top of his head.

Thousands of years from now, an archaeologist of the future will unearth his grave and wonder at the violence that was inherent in his burial, which was obviously not a kind act. What was intended by stuffing the skeletons of rats in the unknown man's mouth? And although he was evidently a soldier, mostly judging by the scraps of uniform lying about, why were his arms so severely bound behind his back? In truth, answers to these questions lie in the Philippine locals' search for vengeance.

When the Japanese military was in control of the situation, some relative had been killed either by shooting (which was actually quite a merciful way to go), bayoneting (a bad way to go if the point of the bayonet entered the gut or higher on the thorax [through the rib cage, to pierce the lungs, or to initiate suffocation if the bayonet point entered the neck area]), or striking with a sword (which caused the victim to bleed to death before he began to feel the excruciating pain, unless the sword was used to decapitate him, in which case the head simply fell off and the entire body leapt forward, usually into a predug grave). Now it was payback time—which amounted to such an extreme act of vengeance.

Reportedly there were thirty thousand Japanese soldiers—most of them members of the Kempeitai group—assigned to Mindanao. Only six thousand of that total were given prisoner of war (POW) status when the war ended, meaning there are twenty-four thousand bodies of Japanese soldiers somewhere on the island or in the sea.

War Story Number Three

Jim Sparks was an enlisted man stationed in the Azores. He was a goof-off doing kitchen police (KP) duty. One day an administrative officer gave him a rifle and said, "It's loaded. You are to sit on these chain mail sacks and shoot whoever comes through that door that does not give you the proper code word. Now I will brief you on the code word. Come with me."

The captain handed him an M-1 Garand rifle as Jim protested his removal from KP duty. The officer insisted: "Come with me. I'll take care of your KP duty. You have far more important things to do now. Come with me." It was an order that even a goof-off would understand.

The captain then took the young man to a covered tin shack next to their runway. All night long, Jim followed orders; he sat upon and diligently guarded the chain mail sacks. Sometime later, he was still curious about the mysterious guarding assignment and asked a high-ranking friend of his in the administrative section, "What was I guarding? What was in those sacks?"

The response was "You were guarding US inputs to Operation Overlord, the overall plan for the invasion of Normandy, France."

Chapter 3

In Between: Growing Up

Retaking the Philippines

After incisive analysis, a noted WWII historian of US Navy operations in the Pacific theater concluded that military phases of the US war plan included invasion of Pacific-theater islands and would eventually lead US forces to the shores of mainland Japan. It turned out that the whole US military effort had been so successful that regaining the Pacific region was ahead of schedule and a Davao City phase was no longer applicable. Japanese military commanders did not believe the news, however, and retained the original numbers of troops in Davao City and Province. Who knows what the effect might have been on the civilian population, including Eddie and Manolo, had Japanese senior commanders believed cancellation of the original US war plans was not another US ruse.

The US invasion of the Philippines, as outlined in special orders and under command of General Douglas MacArthur, originally planned through Davao City and Province, Mindanao, was cancelled in October 1944. Essentially, since US forces had made such progress in the Pacific theater of WWII, the newly revised war plan intended to bypass Mindanao altogether. Japanese military leaders, however, did not believe the US forces could be so successful.

Senior Japanese military leaders had been expecting American invasion forces to land at Talomo Beach then come up the Mintal-Davao Road, west of Davao City and parallel to our elongated Sunny Brook Farm. But US forces did not do this. Instead they struck Leyte, approximately three

55

hundred miles to the north. This was the first step in wresting back the Philippines from Japanese forces.

Return of Our Papa

After he rescued us from the farm and we were settling in to our new home in Davao City, we were able to learn more about what Papa's activities had been during the war. After the December 1941 bombing of Pearl Harbor, he began making his way back to his family from the official inspection tour of schools that had taken him to the interior of Mindanao. He arrived just ten days after Pearl Harbor, but the Japanese occupation of Davao was already complete. Unable to sneak back into the city, Papa returned to the jungle to organize Philippine guerrilla forces. The 107th Mindanao Guerilla Division, the organization that he claims to have founded, was a ragtag group of about ten thousand resistance fighters. His work was so effective and such an irritation to the Japanese forces that before long they offered a bounty for our papa—dead or alive. By the spring of 1943, he was on the run with his division, which was a mixture of Americans and loyal Filipinos.

A collection of old letters sent home to Indiana from the Philippines includes one dated February 29, 1944, with the simple statement "I'm here, safe and sound." The rest of the letter had been deleted, essentially blacked-out, by the censor officer aboard the US Navy submarine that had been supplying guerilla forces in the pitch-blackness of night. He had no way to safely communicate any of this to his family, who were struggling to survive in spite of the war going on all around them. Finally, on May 2, 1945, by now a US Army major, our papa led the first combat unit across the Bankerohan Bridge to liberate Davao City. When he began a desperate but unsuccessful search to locate his wife and children in the city, someone referred him to the farm, which was still in contested territory. Then he heard that we had moved farther inland, but he was unable to determine the exact location of the Devil's Cauldron.

Shortly after our rescue from the farm by Papa and the Americans, and a brief stay at the US Navy depot at Talomo, we were able to settle into one of our homes in Davao City.

Surprisingly enough, many of our personal belongings were still there and available for our use. Someone with human compassion had stored them in a marked closet.

From the period of getting to know our papa again after such a long absence, my strongest memories are of his unique and colorful way of speaking to us. When he reassumed being head of the household, he used to say, "Oh, piffle!" when he became exasperated over something not to his liking. "Poco loco" is a pejorative American phrase invented by American GIs and used to refer unkindly to a person, usually behind his or her back. Soon after the war, Papa used this phrase often. It is incorrect, however, because both words are classified as adjectives, whereas one should be a noun and the other an adjective. Papa had been using the phrase willy-nilly among native Filipinos. Those who knew him would just smile on hearing the misused phrase because they knew exactly what he meant.

*   *   *

Papa used to go into humorous gyrations, pointing an accusatory finger at an unseen Davao mouse (as he called it) for the noise it was supposed to have made, whenever he passed gas. He then would wave his hand behind him, much as if to dissipate a cloud. I found this to be a funny moment whenever it happened—which was on very rare occasions. As an eight-year-old, I learned that any of my papa's scathing expressions about Davao City, Davao Province, or the region used to infuriate Mama, and I suspected even then that these attendant things associated with him were simply done in order to outrage her.

Soon after we were reunited as a family and living together back in Davao City, Papa decided we all should travel for a day of outdoor fun at Talomo Beach, which had been a US Navy depot after the war. We left early one Sunday morning in our US Army surplus six-wheeled all-wheel drive weapons carrier truck. At the beach, Mama and Papa parked themselves on the upper edge with little Becky and toddler Winston. They were all enjoying the sun in their swimming suits. Bob and I were immediately roaming afar to explore the beach.

Bob, who was a good swimmer, discovered where the mouth of the Talomo River entered the sea. I had never learned to swim, but in my explorations I had discovered the exposed wreckage of a landing ship tank

(LST) that had been destroyed by Japanese forces when the US Navy stormed the beach during the war. I was excitedly climbing around on it and became convinced that it wasn't in water that was more than a few inches deep. So I jumped into the water from the protruding end of the LST. It was then that I realized that the water was way over my head. I was drowning! Bob was not in the area by now, but a young woman strolling the beach saw my predicament, jumped right in, and pulled me to safety. Then she went on her way. Mama and Papa never looked my way, and no one was even aware of my close call.

As I was on the beach, recovering from my deep-water fiasco, Bob came up to me wide-eyed and reported, "There is something huge down there! It brushed against my leg!" Bob had met a local friend who was known to be an excellent swimmer; he could swim like a fish, everyone said. Bob continued to tell how his friend had gone out into the water over a mile. When I looked up to where my brother pointed, we could see the swimmer's head bobbing up and down. Suddenly the head disappeared and the swimmer was gone. I had always wondered as a child what thing could possess the force to drag underwater a very strong swimmer—a large human who was very muscular and physically strong. As I grew older, I conjectured that an underwater creature such as a great white shark had pulled the young man under to his death.

In 2013, I learned of Lolong, a saltwater crocodile that had just died, (after being captured in 2011) and was considered a world record holder in size. He measured just over twenty-one feet from tip to tail and was captured just fifty miles up the coast from the Talomo area, where our family outings occurred. Lolong was known to have eaten eight villagers. Finally, I knew what had happened to the swimmer that disappeared from our sight many years ago, solving a mystery that had bothered me all my life.

The episode of this healthy young man haunted me for many years, also because I saw the whole situation as being terribly ironic; he was able to survive unspeakable terrors over a matter of years of Japanese occupation in WWII and then was easily drowned in less than a few minutes after the war was over by a huge and hungry monster of the sea, which wouldn't be able to distinguish between a civilian and a soldier or between one Japanese soldier from another.

Another ironic death involved one of our tenants on Sunny Brook Farm. Benito was a simple, hardworking campesino who was deathly afraid of carabao. And though I was young, I also saw that his fear in turn ominously affected every water buffalo he approached. Every time he was near them, their tenseness and agitation were noticeable. Even if he merely passed by, each beast slowly turned its head to follow his every movement with its eyes inexplicably limned in red.

One day at Sunny Brook Farm, while full of spirit and unbridled energy, I started running on a narrow downhill path while slapping the sides of my legs, syncopating the slapping and popping noises with the thuds of my feet against the ground. My imagination interpreted this as the sound of a galloping runaway horse. Careening downward to the farmhouse through a winding path lined on both sides with shoulder-high cogon, I approached a small gully at the bottom of the hill. As I rounded a bend, I almost ran into Benito, who was frozen in the middle of the narrow path, his fear-glazed eyes fixed uphill toward my thudding sounds. He was a statue of fear!

After a long moment, he came alive, shaking and trembling. He smiled awkwardly with quivering lips. "You should not do that! I thought it was a carabao." But I didn't listen to his admonition, laughing that I had scared him so. Very pale and still trembling, he slowly turned and continued down the hill. I locked in step behind him, pondering his fright. *Yes*, I thought, *I too would be scared if I faced a carabao stampeding down this path, which is lined with cogon so thick I could not have escaped sideways.* Then my conjecturing simply drifted away for the time being.

Every now and then I would reflect upon the day I terrorized Benito on the hillside, and once again I would conclude that he truly feared carabao. I knew they had a hatred of him because of the fear he projected toward them, although I could not determine why this had to be so. Nevertheless, I had a precognition that sooner or later, and in some terrible manner, a leveling of sorts would have to occur between Benito and all carabao in the world.

When the inevitable reconciliation came, it was tragic but also ironic. At noon on a very hot day only a few weeks following our hillside incident, the gentlest of his four carabao gored Benito to death while he was hitching it to a sled. The beast's hooked left horn impaled him in the groin and lifted him off his feet. The panic-stricken animal then tried to shake off the heavy weight that had been so suddenly thrust upon one side of its head. The effect of its unbalanced shaking was not only incomprehensibly painful to the victim but fatal as well, for the horn was simply driven deeper into the mortally wounded rag of a man.

After a superhuman effort of tugging, Benito's frantic wife finally succeeded in disengaging him from the confused animal's horn. He bled profusely as he was laid on the bare, hard-packed ground, which was searing under the tropical sun. Although he was enveloped in an oppressive blanket of midday heat and numbed by extreme shock, he still shivered violently as if from a severe chill.

In the dimming recesses of his mind, I'm sure he regretted how he had finally come to terms with the greatest of all the fears in his lifetime. As his perceptions faded, he vaguely recollected the violence a *dueña* once described to him in his younger days as she studied with troubled brow a prediction she had discovered among some crushed banana leaves in the palm of her hand. Within minutes, Benito died, mostly of shock.

Philippine Civic Action Unit

Our reunion with Papa was short-lived. When the Eighth Army moved to Japan, he was sent with the occupation forces in Seoul, Korea. While there, he helped establish standards for elementary schools. He was eventually reassigned to the Philippines and then resigned his commission as a US Army major in a military police unit. Since employment with the Philippine public school system had officially ended several years earlier when the Japanese occupation closed all schools, Papa began a new career working with a Philippine civic action unit (PCAU).

The Oliver family pronounced the abbreviation PCAU as "PEE-cow," just as Papa did. His unit was designated number 29, which was assigned to the region of Davao City. Other PCAU units were assigned to various regions of the Philippines. This was certainly a job where Papa's proven qualifications were very closely tied to what civic action experts were supposed to do, and that was to normalize the civilian population.

The specific PCAU office where Papa was assigned was the Philippine Alien Property Administration, known in our family as PAPA. We kids had what we thought was a funny saying that we repeated often: "Papa works for PAPA."

*   *   *

One time after the war, Papa went to the clothes hamper at our home, and reached in to retrieve something like a better shirt than the one he was wearing, as I had seen him do several times in the past. Suddenly he shouted and then held his right arm downward, all the time his face showing intense pain. He was holding the lower part of his right arm with his left hand.

"A centipede just bit me!" he cried out, but was barely able to get his words out because of the intensity of the pain he was experiencing. He openly cried, with tears rolling down his face. Within a half hour, I would guess, his right arm had swelled and turned purple. In his mind, going to the hospital for treatment was not an option. At home, he suffered extreme misery for more than two weeks before the swelling and pain finally started going away. At least he didn't have to have the arm amputated, and eventually he regained full use of the tortured limb.

*   *   *

After the war, we attended Palma Gil Elementary School—or at least what was left of it after destruction by the Japanese. There was no electricity, and the plumbing was primitive. It was located just a few blocks from our home in Davao City, and we walked to it daily. Singing the Philippine National Anthem was part of our school routine, and I can still recall most of the words from memory.

Also, while attending the mostly destroyed Palma Gil Elementary School, we used to sing a Philippine children's folk song about a nipa hut; the song is still well-known today. The tune was upbeat and catchy, and we had a good time singing the words as best we could. I think we had a version that had some native Philippine words mixed with some English. Maybe that is just the way we had more fun with the little song.

As kids, we were fascinated with a type of bean pod that grew in our area. We termed the entire bean pod a sword bean because it was shaped like a sword. The end of the bean pods—that is, the pointed end—were so intensely sharp and pointed that it was actually dangerous to play with them. Sometimes the pointed ends would come in contact with the ends of our fingers or wrists, and we would just stand and bleed until the blood coagulated and sealed up again. Then, once more, we would continue the fight with our sword beans. We often emulated swashbuckling pirates swinging from one ship's mainsail to another. I believe we just naturally quit playing with our sword beans, even without discussing what horrible effects we might have experienced, when an accident occurred that involved our eyeballs. But what did we know as kids looking for something exciting to do?

The very first time I saw a live elephant was during a three-ring circus visit right after the war. The circus had come to Davao City from India. Sadly, according to an item that I read in some newspaper, located with the help of a modern-day computer search engine, the organization fielding the circus folded in the mid-1950s because of cruelty to animals. Now, I don't know if this was true or not, but I would thank them for my first look at such a big animal as a live elephant.

One time, soon after the war, Bob and I were walking up the main path that took us through the cogon near the Sunny Brook farmhouse when we heard a frantic fluttering commotion. We looked toward the source and saw the waist-high cogon moving as if a struggle were happening. Both of us wondered what the cause was, and Bob took the lead. We softly and slyly wove our way through the tall grass and finally arrived at the site. We leaned forward to look, parting the tops of the grass ever so slightly, but I couldn't see a thing because I was still so short—and I was behind my big brother anyway. Bob quickly turned his head to me, his eyes large, his face full of fear and panic, and shouted at me, "Run!" He didn't have to shout twice; I was already turned around the way we had come and running as though the devil himself were after me. Bob, who had longer legs because he was older than I, passed me by as if I were standing still. After running like crazy to a safe distance, Bob looked behind him to be sure the path was clear, and then he and I sat down under a tree. He explained to me that he had seen a very large snake that had totally engulfed a *tikling* (a long-legged grassland bird) that had been caught in a bird trap that someone unknown had set. The snake was huge, he asserted. Years later, I surmised that it had been a python that had wandered throughout its hunting grounds and found a tikling that some human had conveniently trapped.

Not long after our snake encounter, I went to a film with Bob. It was probably made in India; I don't know. There was a clip of two cobras, perhaps of the king cobra species, and both had to be at least eighteen feet in length. A woman (though it could have been a man wearing a skirt, which several years later I found to be a common article of clothing among men, especially those who live in northern India) kissed the nose of one of the hooded snakes. Somehow, they would miss her body or her arm whenever they would strike at her. In the process of titillating a nearby audience, which no doubt included the cameramen, she would extend her hand and push against the throat area of the snakes. The simple move caused the snakes to move backward. Cobras are born mean and poisonous, and less than a drop of venom from either of these snakes could have killed her—and I thought even then that the audience was waiting for that—but it appeared that she was in control of the situation. The heads of both cobras were weaving about, but whatever she did caused both snakes to strike at her but miss.

I'm sure, however, that her heart was beating with apprehension when she first entered the arena. I have wondered for almost seventy years if she ever reached retirement age, at which time she would be able to collect her pension.

Time to Leave the Philippines

Eventually administration of the lands (a function of an unsuccessful Japanese war) was coming to an end. Our parents decided their options for continued employment were running out. What was next? Some more time as an employee in the Philippine government school system? Why, it would be a matter of years before any single school that had been destroyed or disrupted by the war would really be ready for students or for enabling teachers to provide a quality education. In the meantime, we kids would be several years older. After a formal disclosure that alien properties were becoming limited in number and Papa's job would soon terminate, the decision had already been made by both of them that the three older kids would return to Akron, Indiana, in the United States, with Papa.

Mama would remain behind to tend to the administration of family investments—Sunny Brook Farm and the two houses that remained in the city.

Then began a flurry of administrative activity to get proper papers initiated to secure the very first passports we kids owned. Appointments had to be made for photographs to be taken, and then there were the airline tickets needed to fly to Manila and reservations to be made for passage on a ship across the ocean to San Francisco, California.

When we departed the Philippines in 1949 on our way to the USA, we three oldest Oliver children accompanied Papa on a Philippine Air Lines C-47 Dakota Gooney Bird about six hundred miles north, from Davao City, Mindanao, to Manila (capital city of the Philippine Islands). I was almost twelve years old, Bob was fourteen, and our little sister, Becky, was ten. I soon realized that my digestive system wasn't prepared physiologically for this kind of travel. Shortly after takeoff, I vomited my breakfast. I cleaned up all the gooey, sticky mess as best I could. After we got to San Francisco, Papa insisted on taking us for a scenic tour on a rail car and I felt miserable and almost vomited my breakfast again. Then we took a Greyhound Bus past Devil's Tower in Wyoming on our way to Indiana, and on this leg of our journey, I spit up my breakfast again. This set the way for my battle with motion sickness, which continued until I cured myself during pilot training many years later.

A big bird joined us as we traveled past Formosa, which is now called Taiwan. We were aboard the SS *General Gordon,* sailing from the Philippines to San Francisco, California. We marveled at the wingspan of the huge bird. "It must have a wingspan of at least six feet," one of my siblings observed. Papa countered, "It's more like twelve feet!" It was a wandering albatross, and it followed our ship night and day, without seeming to rest. Bob went on deck several times to check out the bird, and nighttime or daytime, there it was—always following our ship. "When does it sleep?" I asked Papa, who quickly replied, "Never!"

Many years later, I read about the wandering albatross, which has an average wingspan of twelve feet. We three kids had seen and had as a traveling companion one of the largest birds in the world. The bird stayed with the ship three days. I understand from my references that the bird sleeps while flying.

In the middle of the summer of 1949, Papa and his three mestizo offspring finally reached their destination of Akron, Indiana, in the United States. As our parents had planned, Mama was still back in Davao City, Philippines, and our youngest brother, Winston, now almost eight years of age, had stayed with her to become an assistant of sorts. Papa and the three older kids arrived at the home of Fay R. Hively. She was my dad's mom and was, of course, Grandma Hively to us. She knew her son Gus was coming back to Akron with his family, but she didn't have room at her Corners Farm for four more relatives, three of whom were kids. So Papa's brother Kenneth volunteered to take the three children (Bob, Becky, and me) if Grandma Hively could lodge our papa. The arrangements met everybody's needs, so our lodging was established accordingly.

In a few months, Bob and I joined our papa at the Corners Farm, while Becky remained with Uncle Kenneth; his wife, Mary; and their two daughters (one older and one younger than Becky). It was another year before Mama and Winston finally departed the Philippines and joined our family living at the Corners Farm.

A couple of years after our relocation to Akron, Indiana, the war claims commission sent a letter dated August 15, 1951, addressed to Mr. Reece A. Oliver (my father) of Akron, Indiana (a community so small that the city and state alone were a sufficient address for delivery of mail). It was in regard to WCC Claim No. MC-116738 and awarded me a compensation in the amount of $1,030.83. The letter went on to say that this was for "Imprisonment and/or Internment from 20 December 1941 to 23 May 1945." A second letter dated August 27, 1951, again addressed to Reece A. Oliver as my guardian, verified that the award was specifically made to each of us due to our "Imprisonment by the Imperial Japanese Government." Separate POW numbers were awarded for my siblings Robert and Rebecca. Winston was not included in this prisoner of war designation because of a strange requirement that children had to be ambulatory during the imprisonment. At the start of the conflict, Winston was still in baby clothes and not ambulatory. The fact that he kept growing and learned to walk could not override the fact that he began his wartime experience as a tiny baby.

Akron, Indiana—A New Culture

I experienced some expressions of cultural differences, especially from teachers—to whom we all look for guidance, and who should have known better! Right off the bat, I was impressed by the generosity of the little town's residents, as well as that of my close relatives. I never once experienced any tendency from my classmates to bully me because of racial differences, although I had anticipated my classmates would be the most likely source of bullying. In fact, it was the teachers—the grown-ups from whom we expected answers—who were the sources of racial bullying. Quite naturally, I liked my classmates while at the same time I disdained certain teachers.

Academically, I was subjected to a few tests in a closed room by officials of the Akron school system. I then was enrolled in the seventh grade, at the same level as other kids my age. That's the point at which I began my integration into a new culture. I liked my personal popularity; I was lucky to be voted into a class office every year since my enrollment. This trend continued to my graduation in 1955, the year I was voted president of my graduating class.

Starting school was a real eye-opener for me in many ways. Mr. Shipley was our seventh-grade teacher, and he was wiser than we thought. One time he made the announcement to the whole class, "You can't cry over spilled milk!" He was talking about the sad effects of puppy love—or, as we know it, a schoolboy crush gone wrong. I recall that he got his clue about the issue from a girl who was crying in the classroom.

Then there were the shenanigans that amazed me. Mr. Shipley was out of the classroom for some reason one day. This seemed a good time for my classmate Tom to jump out of a classroom window (we were on the first floor, of course) to retrieve something belonging to him that a classmate had thrown out the window onto the grass outside. Then his classmates wouldn't let him back in the window! He had to run around to the front door of the school building to get back into the classroom! He had planned to do all this before Mr. Shipley returned. Alas, things don't work out exactly as we plan them. Mr. Shipley came back, and Tom was still outside. Soon enough, Tom came back into the room, and Mr. Shipley did a double take. There were some red-faced words exchanged between

Tom and the teacher. This was just my initial exposure to the frivolity and humor that I observed in my classmates.

Living with Uncle Kenneth's family was mostly a quiet time for me. They were a hardworking, kind, and highly religious family. They habitually said grace before every meal—a practice that I still admire in any family. Aunt Mary was thoughtful and motherly, and she attempted to accommodate the new arrivals to her family group. I enjoyed keeping in touch with her over the years. After my own retirement from the air force, Louise accompanied me for pleasant visits to her Akron home, and then finally to a nursing home.

Aunt Mary was a warm Indiana-born-and-bred woman who called me—her half-Filipino nephew recovering from wartime in a faraway island country—her honey bear. After changing the bed linens shortly after we moved in, she confronted me to explain that this was a different world I was living in now. "You don't have to sleep with a knife under your pillow anymore. You are in the United States of America." She was holding my knife, and I actually felt relief after hearing her words. I only hoped she was a person I could trust; this was a new concept for me. She did not return the knife.

One day I was a few miles away at Uncle Kenneth's farm, anticipating the arrival of the usual afternoon train. Even though a matter of miles was involved, I could clearly hear a huge locomotive pulling a very long and heavy train of cars coming to a stop at the Akron railroad station, which I once estimated to be about three miles away. It was on time, and the weather was so still and the temperatures so cold that I could hear the clanging of metal against metal as well as the shouts of people as they exchanged all sorts of meaningful information. So I quickly jumped on my bicycle and pedaled like crazy on the packed-dirt county road toward a small bridge that had been built many years ago to accommodate an unpaved automobile road over the railroad tracks. I must have broken world speed records, because I beat the train to the overpass bridge. My route crossed Indiana Highway 14, which I fairly flew over—illegal, yes, because I didn't come to a complete stop and then look both ways to check for any oncoming traffic; I simply shot through the intersection. Of course, I had ensured the roadway was clear by looking across the fields (all full of soybeans, I think) in both directions while pedaling my bike as fast as

I could. However, I'm sure that it would appear to anyone looking down the state road that a young kid on a bicycle had simply torn through a main traffic intersection.

The train had started from Akron and was heavily chuffing its way eastward while I rushed on my bike to the small bridge, which barely formed an arch over the railroad—just enough clearance so that the train could pass under the country road of compacted gravel. I screeched to a halt and jumped off my trusty bicycle. I then took my position of standing to face the oncoming train, with both hands tightly gripping a ledge on the side of the bridge. With a great deal of fear and trepidation, I watched the steam engine working its way up the tracks toward me; it would soon pass right under me, only a few feet below the bridge. I anticipated being engulfed in clouds of acrid smoke and cinders; it was a fearsome and huge machine, belching smoke and steam.

As the engine approached closer and closer, I realized the train would pass under me with a clearance of only a few inches instead of the several feet that I had thought would be a safe distance. As the enormous steaming engine came closer and closer, I started to have second thoughts about the whole business and to lambaste myself for taking on such a foolhardy plan. Then I found it was too late to change my mind about leaving in a hurry. I was suddenly enveloped in a black, hot, dirty cloud of smoke and cinders. I had never even thought of it before now, but I wondered at that moment if I would suffocate. Would conditions be such that I could die in this unexpected lack of air? Why hadn't I thought of these things before making such a stupid commitment? Sure, it was a commitment to myself, but that didn't remove any second thoughts I was having about the whole idea.

I was torn between abandoning my intention to stay in place to weather whatever came, because I knew nothing bad could really happen—until, in the midst of this choking man-caused hell on earth, the locomotive engineer decided it would be just the right time to blow the whistle!

Well, he pulled the cord. The shriek of the whistle, which had been designed by college graduates to be heard so the track could be cleared several miles ahead of the huge machine, happened just inches from me! I can hardly describe what I heard, because even at such a young age I knew what kind of sound I expected to hear. Instead, I was so close to the source that I could actually feel a vibration in my bones as the siren sounded. Noise is noise, but this was *loud*. I thought I had died and gone to hell!

In my mind's eye, I can still see the locomotive engineer laughing over his creation of a hell on earth for a first-timer kid. He would never know of the consternation he had just manufactured for a youngster bravely watching the monstrously large machine pass just below as he was engulfed and suffocated by the stench of the cloud the engine was belching into the air. Then the kid would be enveloped in hot cinders just as he the engineer pulled the cord for the shrieking whistle. Boy, what a laugh! What a big laugh. I have had many years to think about it. I have remembered details of the event several times and concluded that no one should go through the experience more than once.

Uncle Kenneth and his family were highly religious, and in their home, I was clearly gaining an understanding of the difference between heaven and hell (and my experience with the train from the bridge seemed like a good example of the latter). Nevertheless, I include this story because it has remained very important to me since it happened, as I was only beginning to learn the nuances of a new culture at the time, and because the locomotive engineer's actions gave me a different perspective of a typical adult American—he had a playful sense of humor and whimsy! I had incorrectly expected him to be only very serious-minded, and simply ignore, as not worth recognizing, a small boy on a country bridge. I truly had begun to fear all American adults, because it seemed to me that in this culture they were all like most of my teachers—and even Uncle Kenneth, to a degree: stern, mean, and gruff. After all, they had immediately become definitive examples to me—a sensitive, kind of confused new kid in town. Now, even as I write this book, I am eternally grateful that my impressions didn't come true, and that they remained exactly where I left them that day with the train—behind me as a twelve-year-old.

As I look back, my early years in the United States seem to have a consistent backdrop of the Erie Railroad, whose main line ran through our little town of Akron, Indiana—the sights, the sounds, the stories— the wonder of it all. Papa told me that Erie Railroad locomotives were the largest in the Midwest. I never asked him why they were so large; nor did I ever find out from him before he passed away. But today I believe I have the answer. It lies in the steepness of the Disko grade, a railroad bed incline that was relatively precipitous as far as the pulling capability of a common locomotive was concerned. I still clearly recall relatives telling of Uncle Cecil's terrible death on the Disko grade when the boiler on his locomotive exploded. The accident happened in 1905, and locomotive technology had not yet advanced to enable the locomotive engineer to determine how much water or steam was in the boiler. In Uncle Cecil's case, the engineer decided to inject cold water into the boiler, which the analysis investigators found had been not only hot but very dry as well, and when the steam created by the hot boiler expanded, the pressure that developed was enough to blow up the entire locomotive. Everyone on the engineer's staff aboard the locomotive was killed.

Anyway, the Erie Railroad Company would have incurred an exorbitant cost if the grade had been made somewhat flatter. Miles of construction and hundreds of tons of construction fill dirt would have been involved. It was cheaper by far to buy bigger locomotives that could easily climb and pull a long train up the grade than it would have been to reconstruct the railroad bed so smaller locomotives could be used to haul goods up the Disko grade. Also, during actual fill-in operations, every now and then cross-country vehicular traffic would have to be stopped, and doing that would alienate the public. Moreover, interruption of the Erie's hauling of goods and passengers would put a dent in daily schedules, if not the deliveries themselves. So all in all, costs that the company would incur would have been prohibitive.

We could hear the whistles of trains at the Corners Farm from ten miles away on a cold morning. Regularly, several times every day, we could hear the Erie Railroad train stop in Akron, Indiana. The distance was only a little over three miles, but we could hear it loud and clear. Other regional trains operating near us were the Santa Fe and Monon.

The Monon Railroad was ten miles to the north, and again, on cold mornings, we could hear the whistle. My brother Bob and I would wait for our school bus, and we could hear the Monon trains out there from a long distance. And just about the time I could no longer hear a train and my feet would start to ache because of the cold, sure enough, the school bus would arrive. Once I was inside the bus, with the heater going full blast, my feet would warm up, but throughout it all, I could hear the railroad whistles again. I never took them for granted. I always wondered where the trains might be going.

Soon after I started my first year of school in Akron, Indiana (seventh grade), one of my classmates told me about the local Boy Scout troop, to which he belonged. He invited me to attend the next meeting, that same night. Scouting for me became an opportunity to receive recognition for accomplishments with awards and commendations. I was also fortunate during those years to have two outstanding troop leaders. They were both dedicated to the positive development of troop members and became excellent role models for each of us. One was Scoutmaster Charles Feller, who was the leader of Boy Scout Troop 45. The other was Scoutmaster Paul Schaeffer, who led Explorer Scout Troop 245.

I was highly motivated by Boy Scout standards, activities, and expectations. I earned the Eagle rank as a high school senior in 1955. At that time, there were 105 merit badges, and I completed requirements for 33 of them.

On the back of several worn and faded award and certification wallet cards that I still have is a statement that exactly defines my scouting experience:

> You have advanced another Rank in Scouting,
> and this certificate is given as recognition of
> what you have accomplished. It has taken work,
> but you have had the satisfaction of reaching the
> goal you set for yourself. Now there is a
> new goal ahead—your next Scout Rank.

At age fourteen years and above, I could choose to remain in the regular Troop 45, with brown uniforms, or move into the Explorer program Troop 245, with green uniforms. The highest achievement for an Explorer was the Silver Award. I completed requirements and received that award when I was a freshman student attending Purdue University in 1956. I have not slowed down since.

Another aspect of my scouting experiences led to me being awarded a certificate in recognition of first aid abilities in the County First Aid Team Competition. The award formalized my achievement as a member of our Boy Scout first aid team that took first place (among several first aid awards presented that night) in a series of competitive meets throughout the past year, including competition against a Logansport, Indiana, emergency medical technician (EMT) team. The Logansport EMT group had competed against other EMTs from various counties around the state and had earned first place recognitions by beating other EMTs.

There are three individuals from my Boy Scout years that keep cropping up as being important influences for me: Arden Walgamuth, Bob Hattery, and Charlie Miller. They were also my partners on our award-winning Akron Boy Scout first aid team. It is interesting that in later years Walgamuth became a dentist, Miller became a medical doctor, and Hattery became a medical doctor (and headed up the Mayo Clinic in Minnesota at one time). I became a USAF squadron commander. I guess some of us were cut out for medical careers and some of us were not, no matter how successful we were as a group in our Boy Scout competitions.

During two summers in my high school years, scouting included sessions at Camp Buffalo. This was a summer camp for Boy Scouts of all ages near Monticello, Indiana (about an hour west of Akron). After one year as a camper, I became a staff member and earned certification to be an instructor of such Boy Scout skills as bridge building, canoeing, swimming, and fire starting. It was here that I was inducted into the Boy Scout honor society known as Order of the Arrow. Within a year I became the *Netami Lekhiket*, or lodge secretary.

The Corners Farm

Even though we were back in the USA and our schools were far superior to the dismal attempts at teaching that we experienced after the war in Davao City, the employment situation for Papa was a serious problem. There were no job opportunities in Akron or the nearby areas. At first, he reluctantly moved farther afield and taught night classes at various military installations in Indiana and Ohio, part-time. Then he was able to secure a position at Bunker Hill Air Force Base, near Kokomo, Indiana, as a security guard. He was away from home during the week, only returning to the Corners Farm on weekends during most of my school years in Akron. It wasn't until 1959, when I was a university student, that he finally retired.

I have fond memories of working with Papa on the fences surrounding the farm. It was miserably hard work in the intense Indiana heat of summer. It seems we continually needed to replace rotting fence posts. Papa used a handsaw to cut down an oak tree, and then eventually he split the dried wood with an ax. I was too small to be much help, but I did as much as I could and cherished being around him. From memory, he would recite stanzas of poetry from the works of various classical writers, such as Rudyard Kipling, Percy Bysshe Shelly, or Alfred Tennyson. I can still quote many of the lines myself, but nothing like the endless selections Papa shared with me.

Corn was the main crop at Corners Farm. We also grew some alfalfa, which could be baled. We had New Zealand white rabbits and a barn full of cats and kittens, and dogs and puppies. In Fulton County, it seems our corner where two rural roads intersected had the reputation of being an ideal place to drop off any unwanted pets. One time when I came home on the weekend from college, Papa was distraught. He explained that he had just completed the upsetting process of shooting and burying all the barn dogs. They were starving and there was no food available to keep them alive. He didn't want to see them suffer further.

Bob and I were each assigned a milk cow, and I named mine Gussie (after my papa)—Bob's cow was Bucky. Every day before school, we had to milk our cows. The family attempted to earn some income with a commercial milk operation; but without expensive renovations, it was impossible to meet inspection standards. In my sophomore year of college, I came home one day and was told they had sold Gussie to help finance my schooling. I was upset—mostly because I hadn't been involved in the decision and found out about it only after the fact.

When mama arrived at the Corners Farm, she adopted the areas along the entrance to the house and planted lilac bushes, irises, and many other flowers that are still recognizable today. It was her dedicated attempt to make the area look civilized and lovely. She eventually assumed the companionship and care of household cats, which did not have to struggle for survival in the barn.

One time when I was working with Papa, we saw a snake slithering away from us into the undergrowth. This prompted him to explain (much to my awe and amazement, as usual) that a snake was like a bullwhip, with a flexible, ropelike body and a large head at one end. He taught me that if you grab a snake by the tail and quickly snap it away from you with a strong wrist motion, the head will separate from the body and pop right off.

Sometime later, I was out in the fields and spotted a long garter snake. Remembering Papa's vivid instructions, I didn't give it another thought. I took hold of that snake and gave it a quick snap, and just as Papa had described, the head popped right off the body. Then, as I watched the headless body writhe in the grass and clover, a feeling of regret took over. Then I cried, because it was just an innocent snake, not a poisonous one. After it was too late to change anything, I decided the event was not really fair because the snake was not virulent and would not harm me down on the ground. Then I recalled how its detached head had flown past my right eye. Had it been a much more poisonous type, such as a water moccasin or the like, and its fangs had hit my eyeball, I wouldn't be writing about the encounter today. In essence, a virulent snake would have had a last laugh had its detached head struck my eyeball. I never had the urge to test that technique again, and I continue to be sorry that I even did it that one time.

Now that I brought up the garter snake story, I realize that growing up held other similar regrets for me. I seemed destined to learn some of life's lessons the hard way. One example is the time I was out in the meadow with a rifle, planning on taking a few shots for a little target practice at the end of a busy day. Upon spotting an object sitting atop an iron gate in the distance, I took quick aim, pulled the trigger, and proudly observed that I had judged just right. It looked like I hit the target dead on—truly a remarkable shot! I guess I didn't really think I would be that successful, and I had mixed emotions of dread and trepidation, yet wonder, as I walked forward to check out the results of such skill. When I discovered it was a bluebird as small as my thumb, and I knew they were very scarce, I cursed myself and then cried like a baby. I had just needlessly taken the life of that tiny, beautiful bird.

One bright but chilly Sunday, we all were attending church services in town with our mama. Papa did not attend with us; he proclaimed that Sunday was his day to work on the farm. I am not sure of the year, but Mama was involved, so evidently she had already arrived from the Philippines. We kids were all attentive to the sermon that was delivered by Reverend Donald Clayton, a well-known pastor in the community.

The sermon turned out to be a rather critical and insulting one for our family, as it was regarding "Christianizing the backward heathens of the Philippines ..." I didn't know a single thing about local attitudes or political correctness, as we call it now. I was still an insensitive school kid. But I got the point when all of a sudden, amid a flurry of localized activity, Mama stood up then walked out of the church! A while later, after church services were over, we all drifted out of the building and found her walking down the sidewalk toward us. I could tell by the set of her jaw that she was still angry.

Today I would be sensitive to the fact that the reverend was assuming that he spoke for the entire community of Akron, Indiana. He addressed miscegenation, how backward Filipinos were, and how people of a color different from his white skin had to be suspect. Of course, without realizing it, he had fallen into a hypocritical trap of his own making: he was stereotyping people. He didn't choose to recognize the following facts:

All Filipinos are not backward. In the audience sat my mama, who had been couched in education since she was a child and held a master's degree in English from the University of Chicago; it is possible she was much more educated than the majority of the reverend's flock. I have no doubt that she spoke better English and knew more details of the language than did 99 percent of the reverend's audience. Furthermore, she was raised as a devout Catholic in a Filipino population that had been believers in the teachings of Christ for several generations.

The Philippines as a country has been Christianized since the arrival of Catholic monks in 1520, when they landed with Magellan on Mactan Island. The Spanish explorer died in the Philippines 316 years before Akron, Indiana, was founded in 1836. It is an unfortunate fact that my mama, arriving only recently from the Philippines, with skin of a different color, but had a sincere desire to worship just like the rest of the congregation, was driven to walk out on the Reverend's sermon—she had not understood that she was in the United States of America, one of the most racially prejudiced countries in the world.

Racial prejudice is defined as an irrational, illogical hatred of an individual on the basis of race. Somehow, someway, the very same reverend—although today he would undoubtedly deny everything if he were confronted—had adopted racial prejudice as a daily tenet and found it to be an appropriate subject for a Sunday sermon. Mama had rightfully been offended. The rest of us, who after all were still kids and had already learned to not listen to such inflammatory words, weren't offended, and we stayed in our seats. I have no doubt that if we had understood what the reverend was really saying, we would have accompanied Mama in her departure. I now regret that I did not walk out with her.

I have always appreciated that my classmates and peers genuinely accepted our arrival in their isolated Midwestern community, permitting me to feel no different from any of the rest of them. The adults, however, outside of immediate family members, were not so generous. Our darker skin color and slightly Asian facial features made us *different* and therefore open to racial slurs, unkind references, and hurtful reactions when we were in their presence.

* * *

Let me introduce my Akron High School class. I have often been among total strangers when the subject of high school graduating classes has come up for discussion. I admit that our graduating class was small, with only thirty-seven students in it, but I have determined that by comparison, we were a pretty special group. Tom Phillips, Kent Nelson, and Sharon Miller are three outstanding representatives of my Akron High graduating class—AHS-55—that I have chosen to acknowledge in this memoir. In July 2015 we will hold our sixty-year class reunion at the community center in Akron, Indiana.

Sharon still lives in our high school community and just last summer traveled to visit me and my wife and at our cottage in Michigan—with extensive updates on the latest town events and happenings.

Kent experienced difficult family situations in our senior year, and I've always admired how he was able to keep forging ahead anyway.

Tom was never afraid to go against the grain of what was expected, demonstrating a consistent degree of antiestablishmentarianism on many different occasions through all the years we were in Akron schools together.

I'm taking the liberty of sharing Tom's description of our class. He captures the experience of my years in Akron, Indiana, so completely. Tom writes:

Going to a small country school as we did might have been a hindrance to one's success in life, but in my case, it was a fortunate stroke of luck. Our class was pint-sized, but each member of our group adopted an individual responsibility to make the small bunch special to anyone's eyes. We took on moneymaking projects (for example, planting Christmas trees and harvesting an entire cornfield by hand) in order to plan a special trip at the end of our senior school year. As a matter of fact, we did so well that we were able to take a trip to New York City as well as buy a new water fountain for the school with some of our leftover funds.

In the center of the Corn Belt, in a school surrounded by productive fields, a number of our classmates became successful farmers. A good percentage, however, went on to budding careers as professionals in medical, military, and business areas. Although we as class members have scattered from Arizona to Florida and from North Dakota to Mississippi, all of us still feel a compelling need to return to our roots in Akron, Indiana, for our class reunions. This is best exemplified by the fact that twenty-two of the remaining thirty-one classmates came from all parts of the country for our fifty-year class reunion in 2005.

Many of my friends are awed when I tell them that if a member of our graduating class becomes critically ill, the word quickly spreads to the rest and there is an instant outpouring of concern and love to the afflicted one. Over a matter of months, many of us remain in close contact with one another and with the sick one by computer or cell phone. This has happened because we grew older together, instead of separately and individually. These gestures of concern have helped build my character. My gratitude to my classmates is boundless.

Thanks, Tom, my sentiments exactly—JSO

*   *   *

Velma was the executive officer of the library in Akron, Indiana. She retired after sixty-five years of service in that position, and then, within a year, she died of cancer in 2012. All the local citizenry mourn her passing, but I miss her so much. It was her library that opened the whole world to me. It was her library, her books, that made the world real. And I would later travel to many, many countries and travel many, many thousands of miles to see for myself that the world was indeed real.

Ann Allen was recipient of the 2008 Dunn Award for her comprehensive feature on the history of my father as organizer of the 107th Mindanao Guerilla Division in Mindanao, Philippines, during World War II. She was a well-known Akron, Indiana, journalist, having been dedicated to her work for over forty years. She attended Akron schools in my brother Bob's class, two years ahead of me. It was an honor to have Ann attend the sixtieth Akron High School class of 1955 reunion, and our lunchtime conversations were fascinating. Sadly, Ann passed away just three months later.

Purdue University

After finishing high school, I enrolled at Purdue University in West Lafayette, Indiana. Most of my Oliver relatives went to Indiana University, graduated, and became teachers. I am one of only a few of us in modern family history that went to Purdue University, and I did so mostly because I wanted a degree in aeronautical engineering. However, the realities of my academic abilities sent me in a more appropriate direction to receive a bachelor's degree in international relations.

I had originally dreamed of becoming an astronaut, like Ivan Kincheloe—he was my hero and a Purdue graduate. After all, the National Aeronautics and Space Administration had already named Ivan to be the first man to walk on the moon. At that time, NASA had a policy of naming whoever was going to walk on the moon several years in advance, and Ivan had been chosen. He died in his F-104 Starfighter, however, and about that time NASA changed its policy on naming in advance. That is why Neil Armstrong (by the way, another Purdue graduate) became the first to walk on the moon.

To help pay for the expenses of going away to school, I worked as a laborer on the hot Erie Railroad beds during the summer between high school and college. I was assigned to a crew that maintained tracks and communication cableways from Akron to Rochester, Indiana, westward. We dug cable trenches, laid steel rails, and painted creosote onto oak ties. It was always hot, backbreaking work; I came to the conclusion that there is not one single cool day in Indiana between June and September. The railroad pay was excellent though—$2.96 an hour!

While working on the railroad, I experienced a recurrence of malaria chills. Symptoms included feeling chilled to the bone although the skin on my arms and neck was hot and clammy. I wanted to stay wrapped up in an old US Army blanket—even though the ambient temperature was about ninety-six degrees Fahrenheit. The foremen said I had a case of the "rhubarb chills" (whatever those might be).

I tolerated the heat and hard work since I knew it was necessary to be able to go on to Purdue University beginning in the fall of 1955. During school months, my earnings came from work in the dining halls when classes were finished each day. Tuition at Purdue was relatively inexpensive for me because I was an Indiana resident. One time, when I was able to schedule a Purdue visit for my mama and papa, I was able to save and present to them six paychecks—which, of course, they refused.

Arriving at Purdue, I checked in to my dorm room, located in the Cary residence halls. I brought very little with me, and my wardrobe was only functional and very limited. With some of my hard-earned money from a summer of work on the railroad, I was pleased to be able to buy one new shirt. It made me very proud to have such a nice plaid flannel shirt with a sporty collar, brown buttons, and long sleeves. During the first week, there was the usual orientation meeting scheduled for all the new students, and they noted that casual attire would not be acceptable. I was so pleased to have my new purchase for the occasion—until I arrived at the auditorium. Everyone else was wearing a starched and pressed white shirt—and most of the newcomers to the orientation meeting wore ties with their white shirts! I concluded that I had a lot to learn about life away from the Corners Farm in Akron.

After the reverend insulted my mama during his church sermon, I had my second openly expressed experience with prejudice from a teacher in college. I was the only non-Caucasian in the large class. I could not understand why he mostly called on me, demanding answers—constantly, it seemed. Even several of my classmates came up to me after the bell had ended the session and said, "Why do you take it?" I eventually wound up dropping out of the class, mostly because I thought the teacher hadn't taught me a thing and he was already evaluating me. In my view, there is a distinction that a teacher must draw. He should instruct first, and then, later on, he would be able to objectively evaluate what he has taught. I felt he was evaluating me long before he taught me. Now that I know what I have learned over the years, I would like to meet and have a discussion with that teacher again, but I know I never will. I am certain he has died of old age.

As a new freshman student in town and anxious to try new things, I tried out for an announcer position on the Cary Hall WCCR radio station musical show. For weeks I was disappointed by my failure to qualify. I would hem and haw, and even I realized that I simply did not have a good presence or voice for the radio. Students would write unkind letters to the station asking, "Just who is that *loser* on the show called *Rainbows in Music?*" However, I didn't give up, and I soon successfully found my niche as programmer for the musical radio show. I wrote down song titles and artists that the boss (a senior only a semester away from graduating) reviewed, and then I located the 45 rpm and 33 rpm discs he selected, in the disc library. My work on that radio show made me a winner of the WCCR Silver Key Award. This award was generally presented to a senior or postgraduate member of the staff, and I received my award as a freshman!

After two years of college, engineering math courses were giving me nothing but trouble. So, on the advice of a kindly old professor, I switched to the humanities, and then I made As and Bs in almost every course. Within four semesters of the big switch, I was also selected the cadet division commander of Purdue's 2,200 Air Force Reserve Officer Training Corps (AFROTC) cadets and earned the Military Order of the World Wars Award. A few months later, I had earned enough school credits for a bachelor of science degree in international relations and a commission as a second lieutenant in the US Air Force active-duty reserves.

Spelunking and Other Stuff

Nelson was the president of the Indianapolis Grotto Club. One fall we met at the entrance of a hole in the ground, approximately five miles north of Oolitic, Indiana. Nelson gave us a briefing about the cave his Grotto members were about to enter. I thought all this was exciting.

I thank God that Nelson included a safety briefing, because a fifty-yard section of the cave was so restrictive that it required us to use half-breaths to keep our chests from expanding as they would under normal breathing conditions. Under normal breathing conditions, we would have been able to move neither forward nor backward, because our chests would have been stuck between sand below and a rock roof at our backs. I would have panicked had Nelson not included those instructions in his safety briefing. (I have referred to the place as Half-Breath Cave ever since.)

We got into the cave within a half hour of Nelson's briefing, and I went down and down and down for a long time. I fought insects and spiders all the way. We wore hard hats with carbide lamps attached to them. We each also wore at our waist two canteens, one full of dry carbide and the other filled with water. I carried distilled water that could be used both for drinking and creation of methane gas when combined with the dry carbide. Each of us had a lighter, or we could ignite our lamp from someone else's that was already burning.

Before going farther into the cave, we checked one another's lamps for functionality. Then we all stretched out on our stomachs and started inching forward. We had to take the hard hats with the carbide lamps on them off our heads and push them in front of us so we could have some light. The first person, who was the leader of the exploratory group of about a dozen of us, called back after a while and said, "Here is where we start taking half-breaths!" I was in a quandary; it was too late for me to say that I could not continue. I was going to tough it out with the rest of them.

After what seemed a long, long time, the leader of the group called back and said, "I can breathe again, I can take full breaths." He asked, "Did any of you see any mud?" We answered one by one that we had not seen any mud. (He was trying to determine if this was a wet cave or not. Sometimes, when thunderstorms occur miles and miles away, water will rush through a wet cave.)

I turned toward a wall of stone, turned off my lamp, and placed my left hand in front of my face. This was my test to see if there was any other source of light. I could not see my fingers. "We're down here, all right," I said to myself. The passageway we had just traversed opened up into a large room, and each of us went our separate ways. I was surprised at the alacrity and boldness of our leader and his henchmen, who had evidently run across the large room and were already hunting new passageways. It was then that I had decided I was going to become familiar with my present environment before I hunted new venues. (Many years later, I would apply the same approach; whether it was US politics or the discovery of a new flower, I would study the one I had discovered before I made the effort to find another.)

Nelson stayed close to me because he knew that this was my first cave. Besides, he did not have the same inclination as the others. Right at my feet were two puddles cut into the rock. In one puddle was a shrimp, and the other contained a fish. Both had no eyes. (Of course they would not have eyes! They had absolutely no use for eyes in the pitch-black cave.) I made a drawing of the fish and the shrimp with a pencil on a piece of notepaper that I carried.

The room of the cave was huge! The beam of my carbide lamp could not even reach another wall. I studied the fish for a while, and then moved to the shrimp. It was facing in the same relative direction as the fish, and it too had no eyes. (I knew from my young days during the war that shrimp eyes were at the ends of two stalks that protruded from the head shell.)

Suddenly my ears popped. "Hey, Nelson," I called out, "did your ears just pop?"

He replied, "By God, they just did!" He immediately turned around and shouted, "Hey, guys, our ears just popped. Everybody collect here right now!" I could hear some grumbling, but they obeyed in a disciplined manner, and pretty soon the group was gathered around the president. He pointed at me and said, "His ears popped just as mine did, almost simultaneously. That means our room is filling up with water. Now, ASAP, let's get the hell out of here!" There was only one cave opening for entering as well as exiting, and we knew we had to go through our half-breath portion again, except this time we were in a hurry. In fact, we were panicked. The exploratory leader was first, and he brazenly forged ahead.

I was number three in line, practically the same position I had been in when we first entered the cave a few hours before. I churned away and had somehow gotten through the half-breath portion of the cave when a voice from above me said, "Hey, fella. Up here." Otherwise I would have gone in the other direction! I clambered vertically up toward the voice until I could finally see the opening. I have never, ever been so glad to see the light of day again. I was surprised to hear a lot of grumbling when the group gathered around Nelson, all because the day exploring the cave had been cut short.

"Hey, guys," Nelson said, "better to be red than dead. I'll see you next week."

Two weeks later, I saw Nelson at Cary Hall, back at Purdue University, and I said, "You know, Nelson, I've never had a chance to thank you for your leadership at our Half-Breath Cave. Are you interested in exploring the depths of Cary Hall?

Nelson dismissed my appreciation with a wave of his hand and said, "I've been meaning to ask somebody about the prospect of exploring Cary Hall's innards. It might as well be you. I'll see you down here at nine o'clock tonight."

I was delighted. I prepped by getting a new battery into my US Army crooked-neck flashlight, and I put on my grungiest clothes because I knew it was going to be dusty. Sure enough, at nine o'clock that night I met Nelson at the end of the stairway and told him he was the leader. He immediately wore the mantle of being in charge and looked left and right. Seeing no one to object to our plans, he crawled through a little doorway adjacent to the stairway. It was immediately pitch-black again, but this time I did not do my usual test of placing my hands in front of my face and wiggling my fingers. Nelson was a good leader. We went down into the basement of Cary Hall, which turned out to be a much larger complex than I had ever imagined.

After a long while of playing follow the leader, Nelson said, "There is a manhole above us, and I'm going to take a peek." I was starting to get bored with following my leader, a voice in the darkness. He then climbed up a short ladder and lifted the edge of the manhole cover. As soon as he lifted the edge of the cover, we were flooded with the sounds of partygoers' voices coming from above. We were at the Snake Pit! How we got there so fast, I don't know. (The Snake Pit was named after a popular movie that starred a budding Hollywood starlet; it was a favorite after-hours gathering place for PU students—even though alcoholic drinks were not allowed.)

We doubled back and headed for the Cary Hall stairwell access once more. At least that is what Nelson told me we were going to do. If anyone had asked me where I was, I wouldn't have been able to say with any accuracy.

In the dark, we stood on some steel grating. I could hear dirt falling into water way, way below. I broke out my crooked-neck flashlight and studied where our feet were placed. I had never seen anything like this; the steel grating was bending under our weight. I could see shiny metal through the bending rusted outer surface. It was about to break! Had we broken through, our ankles would have been trapped by rusting iron.

"Hey, Nelson," I warned, "we've got to find some concrete right now." Nelson was a slight, scrawny guy, while I was thicker and denser than Nelson and would have broken through first.

Still, he twisted immediately and said, "Over my right shoulder—there's some concrete!"

I sat and then rolled over in order to distribute my weight more evenly. "That was a close one," I observed. "We could have screamed our heads off for years, and no one would have heard us!" Nelson agreed.

We gingerly walked along the concrete edge. Finally Nelson said, "Here we are, back where we started." How we got there, I'll never know. We scurried through the doorway and were able to look each other over. We were coated with years of accumulated dust and needed a shower badly. I looked at my watch and saw it was just after midnight. We had spent three hours down there. I am now seventy-eight years old, and I have not gone spelunking or exploring under old buildings at any time since then.

Graduation—BS in International Relations

In January 1960, at my graduation from Purdue University, the professor of air science said, "A bachelor of science degree comes with the commission, you know." But the message was not what the PAS meant. He meant to say, "A commission as an air force officer comes with the bachelor of science degree," meaning that a BS degree would be conferred by the university upon the student after four (and more, in my case) years of hard work. Then the message from the PAS would have been meaningful. All in all, I passed this off to his excitement and pride—for me, too—for 2,200 cadets in his command! I was proud, too, having just been appointed division commander of all those cadets. A few weeks later, I was also awarded the Medal of the World Wars, from the Chicago Tribune group.

After I graduated from Purdue with a bachelor of science degree in international relations, I took a temporary job at US Steel in Gary, Indiana. I also had a commission as a USAF second lieutenant, but I would not report for duty until six months later. This meant nothing to the employment office at the big steel company, and my first job was to clean the men's restroom. (I think this was punishment for not joining their union. Nonetheless, I put forth my best effort, and you could have eaten off the restroom floor!)

After a few days, I was moved to a new entry-level position: cutting up scrap metal with a torch. On my first day I was introduced to an artist-type old-timer who had spent thirty-five years doing the same work in this department. He was proud to show me how to carefully cut the metal in such a way that the same tanks of acetylene and oxygen would last all day long. Not me. I used to go through many tanks of either acetylene or oxygen every day. The molten metal used to fly by my face in flaming droplets. I was not an artist; nor did I intend to stay for thirty-five years doing the same thing!

We worked in a large, unheated industrial building. It was cold outside (and in the early months of the year, near Lake Michigan, it was always cold), so I routinely dressed for warmth and wore a hooded sweatshirt. One day, my coworkers came in a swarm, running toward me and shouting, "You are on fire!" Apparently one of those flaming sparks had landed on my hood, and I didn't know it. Eventually I would have known about my burning sweatshirt hood, but until the other workers came shouting toward me, I didn't have a clue that I was in trouble.

I quickly shucked out of the damaged sweatshirt, and I couldn't wear it the rest of the day because of big burned holes in it. You would think US Steel would have an extra jacket somewhere, but no, I had to take sick leave to go home and get some other warm clothes. In spite of the damage to my sweatshirt, I was not injured—I just lost a precious afternoon of pay.

*   *   *

Don Krekelberg, USAF (retired), and his wife, Dorothy Mae, used to live in Lafayette, Indiana. He was my mentor in the Air Force Reserve Officer Training Corps at Purdue University. Over my twenty-four consecutive years of military service following commissioning as a second lieutenant, I considered Colonel Krekelberg an especially strong influence in my life. I easily recollect the moral support he gave me during a period of four and a half years of Purdue classes I took to earn a bachelor of science degree in international relations.

I mailed Colonel Krekelberg a note in which I requested permission to use his name in a section of my book. The letter came back a couple of months later with a US Postal Service annotation on it: "Addressee Deceased." I realized that it is probably a common human frailty to procrastinate while believing that the person to be honored will live forever.

Return to sender. I was shocked. I know that everyone will be affected by old age eventually, but I just hoped to have a chance to explain that he was such an important influence to me. He was an excellent individual, and now he's gone forever. I include Colonel Krekelberg's name as a memorial to the concerned US Air Force officer who influenced me in so many positive ways when I was just a young, struggling AFROTC university student.

Chapter 4

The Cold War: A Blue-Suit World

My US Air Force Career Gets Under Way

In January of 1960, Mama pinned my second lieutenant commissioning bars on the epaulets of my uniform when I graduated from Purdue University with both a bachelor of science degree in international relations and a commission as an officer in the US Air Force. I was so proud of my latter accomplishment that, more than fifty-five years later, I still have those second lieutenant insignia bars that Mama pinned on my jacket.

As I was entering into a US Air Force career, my first choice was to become a pilot, and I traveled to Florida with my wife and baby to start primary flight training at Graham Air Base near Marianna, Florida. Pilot training in Graham AFB began in June 1960. Part of the check-in process was to line up half-undressed in our boxer shorts. When I was finished with my medical exam and was leaving the flight surgeon room, going past the lineup of others still waiting their turns, I told them, "Watch out for the medical staff man with the square needle aiming at your left testicle!" I remember personally getting quite a kick out of creating such high anxiety for candidates still waiting in line as they looked at me in confused horror. My career was under way, for better or worse!

Pappy was one my early flight instructors, and we were in a Cessna T37 Tweety Bird, flying out of Graham AFB. It was an orientation flight. Among several areas we visited on this extensive flight, he took me over Tallahassee, Florida. He said, "See that spot on the right?" He indicated the direction with his nose. There was definitely a spot on the ground below us, to the right. "That is where, just last week, an aviation cadet flew his plane into the ground. He was trying to impress his girlfriend."

My thought was, *What a perfectly good airplane he messed up.*

Pappy continued his story. "The locals are still picking up the pieces of his body. I'm going to be your flight instructor; do you have any questions?"

No questions from me. As far as I was concerned, I was just happy the cadet hadn't become an officer! In the process of making a bad decision, an officer candidate had messed up a perfectly good airplane.

My first flight with Pappy was an introduction that I will never forget. He was excellent as a teacher. He would not become an evaluator, however, until just the right moment. Many instructors create a dichotomy they would like to avoid. After dedicated teaching efforts, to also be an evaluator they must be able to answer the question, Does the young man get it, and how do I evaluate his progress? This happens to be the teacher's dichotomy: At what point does a teacher become an evaluator?

During primary flight training, my partner on a dual-solo was a German cadet named Dietr. We had flown our T37 Tweety Bird to the Aerobatics Flight Area because we had been authorized to accomplish simple aerobatics. When we got to the area and the proper altitude, I cleared left by banking and clearing left, and I cleared Dietr's side by banking right. He looked and said, "We're clear here."

I looked at him, and he looked at me and smiled. "Here we go," I said.

Just then, so close that I could have reached through the windshield and touched the hot exhaust, an airplane filled my whole windshield! Another T37 had just completed his loop and dropped down in front of us. He never knew he had experienced a near miss. Dietr looked at me. His face was pale. I looked at him, and visions of a fireball in the middle of the sky flashed through my mind.

No more aerobatics for us. We immediately departed the area, landed, and reported the near miss to our instructor. Pappy just shrugged and said, "That's the breaks. If we reported every near miss incident at a student training base, the air traffic control guys would go nuts!"

I have had years to review my incident. I do not know what happened to Dietr. I also know that there were no other reports of a near miss, so I am convinced the other pilot didn't know he had a near miss. Had he relaxed his grip on the stick of his plane, he would have bored right through the cabin of our T37 Tweety Bird. And there would have been a big flash in the sky, and parts of our airplanes—as well as parts of our bodies—would have fallen to the ground.

I successfully passed all course requirements of the program for primary flight training at Graham Air Base. In 1961, I progressed to the next phase of pilot training when I was assigned to the six-month-long Basic Flight Training Program at Reese AFB, Texas—the 3501 Flight Training Squadron. I flunked out of the flying program on cross-countries. Basically, I could not make my reports verbally and figure real-time data on my knee computer (it was called an E6B)—at the same time. Five pink slips in a row from the instructor was what was necessary to fail, and I earned all five.

Two weeks later, all my classmates graduated with their wings insignia pinned above their left pockets, indicating they were graduates of the US Air Force Flight Training Program. The silver wings glistened in the sun, and a prouder bunch you have never seen. They were mostly lieutenants and captains, and I was very envious of their achievements!

I remember thinking, when I received those five failure slips, that it was the end of the world as far as my career in the US Air Force was concerned. What would I tell my parents? What would I tell my wife and young family? And more importantly, what could I do in the civilian world, given my qualifications? I was bitter about the whole business and became cynical and angry—though I don't know at what or at whom. I thought that Bunker Hill Air Force Base, in Indiana, would be my probable destination, so I primed myself for the trip. At least from there I could find transportation to the Corners Farm. I would just drop in to say hello. But no, after I had prepared myself for the worst outcome, I should have known the Air Force would have other plans for me!

When it became evident that I would not complete basic flight training, I was given a choice of other assignments. They wanted navigators; however, my choice was intercontinental ballistic missiles (ICBMs). Within three months, in the late fall of 1961, I was sent from a US Air Force base in Texas to Vandenberg AFB in California for operations training in ICBMs. I was assigned to the 4315th Combat Crew Training Squadron (CCTS), which was one among the many units permanently based at Vandenberg AFB.

The 4315 CCTS trained every crewmember assigned to the missile fields, as we used to call them, in missile launch and maintenance procedures. I was fascinated with the details and technicalities of ICBMs.

Minuteman—An Excellent ICBM

I learned that liquid propellants, used by earlier missiles, are a mess. One liquid is an oxidizer, and another is the propellant. It is hypergolic (lights spontaneously) when the oxidizer is mixed with the propellant liquid. Thus, the Atlas F and the Titan I and Titan II had separate tanks to hold the oxidizing liquids. Whether the Titan I oxygen-providing oxidizer tank was hypergolic is unknown to me, but it had to carry its own source of oxygen in a separate tank.

The Minuteman, on the other hand, used a solid propellant, carrying its own oxidizer in the mix that made up the solid propellant, and therefore a piece of the propellant could burn underwater. The Minuteman weapon system could be stored miles from human observers, and the system itself relied upon electronic security to maintain its integrity. In other words, the whole ICBM could be stored practically indefinitely. All we had to worry about was a human interfering with the stored ICBM, and remote security subsystems would take care of that problem.

The stored ICBM in its launch facility (LF) had an outer-zone and inner-zone security subsystem. The OZ would detect movement above ground, and the IZ subsystem would detect movement belowground level. Violation of either the aboveground area or the belowground area would result in an alarm at the Launch Control Center (LCC) console of either the missile combat crew commander (MCCC) or the deputy missile combat crew commander (DMCCC). The US Air Force police sleeping upstairs would be called by telephone and instructed to go to the site that had sent an alarm. Two of them would respond, and they would jump in their pickup truck to drive to the affected site. They were both armed with M16s, and typical police procedures would be followed.

The type of OZ and IZ interference the police responded to was varied, but it always merited a full response by humans. Sometimes an alarm was the result of activity by a burrowing rabbit or a hungry coyote. Other times the problem would be human political protesters. The military police were trained to handle problems of any kind.

In the development of the Minuteman system, the most important message that the missile combat crew (MCC) could receive was the order to launch missiles. Such an order would be received as an alphanumeric code, which could be delivered in any sort of manner. (There is no such thing as a fail-safe system that would make it possible to cancel a misguided ICBM once launched, as Hollywood would have you believe.) In the process of launching our ICBMs, we expected incoming rounds from the enemy.

A sensitive command network test (SCNT) was run periodically, and it collected data from the entire system. At this time, each squadron command post (in my case, the SCP was Echo LCC) would collect computer-created data on rolls of paper; this would be analyzed by engineer representatives of the weapon system manufacturing company. The engineers were mostly looking for unexpected defects in the communication capabilities of our system. (Also, we were suspicious of computer hackers even then, and the time frame was 1968–1969.)

After my initial missile training at Vandenberg, I was assigned to the Forty-Fourth Strategic Missile Wing (44 SMW) in South Dakota, and while there were continual improvements to the Minuteman weapon system, including changes in the series of ICBMs, I write this from the perspective of being assigned only to the 44 SMW and having worked with the Minuteman-F ICBM. In my USAF career, there were several changes to the Minuteman ICBM.

USAF Operations and Maintenance

Even though my career began in US Air Force pilot training programs that I failed, my career definitely changed in a positive direction when I was assigned to ICBMs—first operations, and later maintenance. Then I realized that before any major decisions are made about a career, an officer candidate dedicated to the US Air Force mission must decide for himself or herself, whether or not he or she is going to be a maintainer or an operator of a weapon system. As I look back on the start of my military career and the move away from pilot training, I have learned also that a person's dreams must match his capabilities.

I'll explain further with an example. Let us look at a spear. A spear has a point, and the head of the spear is for killing. The operations people are the ones who implement the point of the spear. Maintenance, on the other hand, maintains the point of the spear.

When USAF operations implement the spear, the objective is to kill people, and USAF operations implementers understand that a show of force is necessary. Depending upon the sophistication of the enemy, a show of force can be historical or it can be a surprise.

There is just so much that operations can accomplish in keeping the point of the spear ready for use. An inspection by the operator will usually determine the sharpness of the point of the spear. After all, it is the user of the instrument who will determine its day-to-day readiness. This is where maintenance comes in. Specialists in maintaining the point of the spear schedule the spear for an evaluation and upkeep. Upkeep may even require removal and replacement of the spear point itself.

As matters and history turned out, my military career assignments made it possible for me to be both an operator and a maintainer of weapon systems. Early on, I wanted to be a military officer so I could have more freedom to control my circumstances, so my first decision was to go to college and get a degree. I reached those milestones when I graduated from Purdue University with a degree and an air force commission. I was then in a position to make desired career choices over the years ahead.

*   *   *

I spent eight years in USAF ICBM operations in California and in South Dakota. In 1967, my US Air Force career moved ahead another step as I left the Vandenberg AFB Training Squadron (4315 CCTS) to join the missile combat crew members of the Forty-Fourth Strategic Missile Wing at Ellsworth AFB, South Dakota. A significant number of my compatriots in the missile fields of South Dakota had been my students at Vandenberg in recent years. My arrival in South Dakota felt like an old home week, with many familiar faces.

"Standboard" was the term widely used by rated officers (those who had successfully completed a major flying program and wore silver wings above the left pockets of their uniforms). The standardization and evaluation group at Ellsworth AFB was an adjunct of the ICBM force of the Forty-Fourth Strategic Missile Wing organization—with the responsibility of evaluating our missile combat crew members and maintaining satisfactory performance levels. After a couple of years at Ellsworth AFB, when I was assigned to be a member of the standardization unit, I learned firsthand about the efforts of the group to keep young captains and lieutenants continually between the covers of their operations technical orders—three-ring binders that contained procedures for operating the Minuteman series of ICBMs. Otherwise, the poor guys would have frequently been between the sheets with their latest conquests, worrying more about their waning testosterone levels than the aggression of flights of the Bear and Bison (North Atlantic Treaty Organization [NATO] names assigned to strategic bombers of the Union of Soviet Socialist Republics [USSR] carrying thermonuclear payloads and coming from the north).

In 1970, I accepted a special assignment with the US Army, which included training at Fort Bragg, North Carolina. Then I was sent to the Vietnam War for a year. When I came back from Vietnam, I was first back at Ellsworth AFB and was then transferred to Malmstrom AFB in Montana. This was where I made another career change to ICBM maintenance. After a few months doing ICBM maintenance in Montana, I was reassigned to Offutt AFB near Omaha, Nebraska, as an ICBM maintenance inspector on the Headquarters Strategic Air Command (SAC) ICBM Inspector General Team. I spent two years at SAC Headquarters in Omaha.

Then, in 1978, I was assigned for the second time to Ellsworth AFB, South Dakota. I became the maintenance supervisor of the 44 OMMS and then became the maintenance control officer (MCO) of the 44 SMW. Only a few months later, the 3901 SMES at Vandenberg AFB in California was shopping for a deputy missile maintenance officer, and I got the job, which meant another permanent change of station (PCS). I was in that position for the next two years, and then I was reassigned as commander of the 90 OMMS at F. E. Warren AFB near Cheyenne, Wyoming.

In 1984, after twenty-four years of active duty as a military officer, I retired out of Wyoming as lieutenant colonel as well as ICBM maintenance squadron commander. I moved into a townhouse in Denver, Colorado, because I didn't want to mow lawns or shovel snow.

The Cold War was still in progress when I left the USAF for a civilian job as a logistics representative with Martin Marietta Aerospace Corporation in the MX strategic missile program. My military career spanned from January 1960 through January 1984—almost twenty-four years. In that period, I experienced twelve changes of residence.

*   *   *

Early in my career, I had the nickname of Ice Man. Nicknames were common in the military culture, so I wasn't surprised and was not offended. The Merriam-Webster Dictionary defines "iceman" (one word) as one who sells or delivers ice. But I do not recall ever selling or delivering ice. I explained this to anyone who questioned me about the nickname. In other cultural references "ice man" (two words) is an individual who carries along with him an air of iciness or lack of approachability. This is the work-center nickname I had been ascribed.

I think I received this nickname in the late 1960s from the MCCMs of the Forty-Fourth Strategic Missile Wing at Ellsworth AFB, South Dakota. At the time, I had become a member of the standardization and evaluation group, an adjunct of the ICBM force of the Forty-Fourth Strategic Missile Wing organization.

Several years earlier, however, during my flight training at Reese AFB in northern Texas, we had an open distribution system in which messages of a routine nature could be addressed to the R-Man or the S-Man (the latter of which was me) of the same Oliver surname. As matters turned out, there were two Olivers assigned to the same flight-training unit at Reese AFB: in Texas, one named James Richard Oliver; the other, me, James Stanley Oliver. So messages sent to the R-Man went to James Richard Oliver, and those messages destined for James Stanley Oliver wound up on the desk of the S-Man. I admit that it's a long stretch, but this could be where the name Ice Man originated.

Another possibility for the nickname is that after divorce number one, I ran around with a little group of warriors. At the time, they were young, a large majority of them divorced, as I was, or not married at all. (Much may be written about the adventures we shared, but the telling of those tales is another project yet to be assigned.) One time, at the officers' club bar at Ellsworth AFB, the informal leader of our group took me aside with a twinkle in his eye, and remarked, "You know, Ollie, our group was just watching you stagger off to the men's room, and we've concluded you're definitely an ass man, not a breast man as we first thought." I bought him another beer, and everyone had a good laugh after I replied with a quick rejoinder for times such as these: "Well, I've always thought that a person should learn a lot more from hindsight than from foresight."

War Story Number Four

Major H. told me that he would be a major for the remainder of his career. I responded, "I feel a story coming on. I'll see you after work at the bar." We were at Vandenberg AFB as ICBM procedures instructors assigned to the 4315th Combat Crew Training Squadron. The story he told me raised more questions than anyone had answers for.

He was a navigator on a B-47 Stratofortress that was returning from a Chrome Dome 1 mission. I could imagine him as the navigator on that plane, isolated in a metal box with all the instruments and gauges. He would have had no physical access to either the pilot or the copilot, who had the ranks of captain and first lieutenant. Therefore, Major H. was highest-ranking man on board—even though the pilot was the combat crew commander.

The bomb bay was loaded (a nuclear bomb on board), and the plane was headed back to Bunker Hill AFB, Indiana. It had been replaced by another plane in the Chrome Dome 1 formation. "Why are you so low?" Major H. asked the captain over the internal communications system. He heard a giggle in the background, and knew it was the copilot. The captain responded, "Well, Nav, sir, we're going to fly this big hooter under the Mackinac Bridge!" Major H. told me that he had a chance to look left and to the rear of the airplane, out the window of his cubbyhole, and there he saw the left wingtip tank skipping over the tops of waves.

"No, no," said Major H. emphatically. But they did it anyway. An alert automobile driver on the well-traveled bridge connecting the Upper Peninsula of Michigan saw the B-47 coming at him and could read the tail numbers on the Air Force plane as it flew below him. The driver knew where to call. When the plane landed, there was a committee waiting for them. Two security police were ready for them too. The committee told them, "You aren't going anywhere; there is a court martial coming up for all three of you!" All three crew members were then marched to the brig.

At the court martial hearing, the historic US Army legal case of Major Reno (who in 1876 was fighting for his life and yet was given a court martial for letting General Custer die during battle) was cited and used as justification for punishing Major H. Reno was punished in spite of the fact that he was three miles away from the actual Battle of the Little Bighorn, where Custer was fighting and lost his life and his entire command. Unfortunately, Major Reno just happened to be the ranking man on the scene. This was the same reasoning used against Major H.—the ranking man on that deviant B-47 flying under the Mackinac Bridge in upper Michigan!

Observations and Encounters

At Ellsworth AFB, I developed an understanding of the subtle differences between kinetic and potential energies. Ellsworth was a big organization. It had two wings assigned to it: the Twenty-Eighth Bomb Wing and the Forty-Fourth Strategic Missile Wing. The whole base couldn't help but be a headache to the Kremlin. I realized that EAFB SD was a potent force against the USSR. Obviously each of these groups performed an important function, contributing to the military effort of the USA—but in very different ways. I saw this as a contrast in type of energy involved.

In my view as an MCCC, kinetic energy was the noise associated with the eight jet engines of the B-52 Superfortress. When finished with a mission, the bomber announced its return with the noise of its jet engines, which represented, in my view, a clarion call that signaled its arrival back home.

By comparison, while I was on duty for the Minuteman weapon system, we were working with potential energy, which was the turning green of the lights representing the ICBM. We were monitoring the status of a day-to-day ICBM that was ready to go right now and could strike its target within thirty minutes!

*   *   *

Soon after I was assigned to Ellsworth, I was on my first tour of duty at D-01 Launch Control Center. All LCCs were advised by the Squadron Command Post (Echo LCC) that a weather system was coming in and we would have a lot of snow dumped on us. Everybody and his brother got busy on hearing that we were going to experience an imminent snowstorm. The rancher to the south of us was not advised, however, and his wife was still out walking the fence line.

The first snowflake appeared in the early evening, and only fifteen minutes later, the locals declared that we had a whiteout. The rancher's wife was caught in a full-blown South Dakota blizzard. She had sense enough to keep moving along the fence line until she got to a corner, and then staying there.

This was the first time I had pulled duty at Delta LCC. When the rancher notified us of his missing wife, I immediately alerted the security team on duty. The security police, two of them, were quick to react. On its very last pass, the USAF security truck, with two reaction force members in the cab, was contacted via VHF radio and told to patrol the fence line one more time. As the truck approached the fence corner, the security agents spotted a mound covered with snow. The truck's wheels started to slip and slide.

"I think I see a mound covered with snow," the passenger-side security man said.

The driver replied, "Well, you'd better see something worthwhile, because we are slipping and sliding. Remember: you see it, you inspect it."

I recorded all this in the LCC log. All conversation was to be recorded in the book—especially VHF traffic. All the security people could do was ask me for directions, because I was stuck in the LCC. I replied by VHF, "Be sure to let me know what you are doing."

At the end of the conversation, he said, "Roger."

As matters turned out, the snow-covered mound was the rancher's wife. We can speculate all we want, but those two air force security personnel, without hesitating, risked their own lives in order to find the missing woman. There was a local celebration a week later, and the US Air Force got a lot of credit for saving the life of the rancher's wife. The blizzard raged for three more days, as I recall.

That was my first tour at this LCC, which was located in an isolated location (as usual) about five miles from Wall, South Dakota. My Deputy MCCC and I were in the hole of Delta LCC, which had a special distinction. It was about 125 feet deep—not the normal 65 feet or so. During construction, the excavators found an underground river! Oh, it had a flow, all right, but the civil engineers sealed off our elevator shaft, let the river flow around it, and dug sixty feet deeper. Many years later, Delta LCC was converted into a national monument, so anyone who visits Badlands National Monument may also have a chance to see what a Minuteman LCC looks like!

I was pulling duty in the remote open spaces surrounding Ellsworth AFB, South Dakota. Since the Juliet-10 launch facility (LF) was open for maintenance, the guard was topside, where he was supposed to be. Suddenly he started hysterically reporting over VHF, "It's right above me! It's watching us!" I immediately called the facility manager to the phone.

"Who have we got?" I asked him, by way of determining if we could receive further assistance.

He replied, "Oh, we've got tons of people!" He rattled off the name, rank, and organization of each person who had declared RON (remain overnight) status—including a lieutenant the FM said was commander of a security police squadron.

Selecting the security commander, I replied, "Well, get his a—— up; he can go out to see for himself what his boy is up to out there. He needs experience anyhow!" I could tell the facility manager, who was an enlisted man, would be delighted to wake up the lieutenant.

Upon being called as requested, the lieutenant got going quickly, jumped into an available truck, and drove out to Juliet-10. I had instructed him to contact me on VHF. Finally he came through: "I'm out at Juliet-10," he reported, "and I have quieted down my boy. And yes, it's up there watching us!" I realized this response from the LCC wasn't appropriate, but I didn't dwell on it too long.

I replied, "You too? What have you been smoking, lieutenant?" Three hours or so later, the maintenance team had finished its work and headed back to the base. Juliet-10 was going to be a long-term patient. There was something else wrong with it.

The lieutenant came up on VHF once more. "Sir," he said, "I need some guidance. The thing is still up there, and it appears to be watching us. I have a log also, and what should my entry be?"

I told him, "Lieutenant, have you ever heard of the story of the Roman guard named Horatio? Are you ready to fall on your sword over your log entry? You will do nothing that disparages the Forty-Fourth Strategic Missile Wing. You have no proof unless the UFO pilot bites you on the ankle and we can match his teeth marks; then we can measure them to the UFO pilot's teeth! Only then do we have proof!" The lieutenant must have understood and comprehended my comments, because I did not hear any mention of a UFO incident at Juliet-10.

Several years earlier, I had another personal UFO sighting. I had picked up my three young children in Lubbock, Texas, to stay with me for the summer months. Instead of going back to Vandenberg AFB in California via Highway 66, I had decided to go by Highway 60, which would take me easily through New Mexico and into the middle of Arizona. At a town in Arizona called Snowflake, the highway goes only northward to Flagstaff, Arizona. There is no other road except northward to Flagstaff and then westward to Los Angeles.

It was dusk, and I stopped for a break at a roadside park—one of several along the way. A movement in the distant colorful sunset caught my eye. Then one of the kids woke up and closed the car door. It was Karin, all five years of her. "What cha doin', Dad?" she asked.

My response was not earth-moving: "Just watching UFOs."

She joined me, and together, in rapt fascination, we observed the wondrous show. Off in the distance, perhaps many hundreds of miles away, two balls of blue light were bouncing up and down. I don't know what they were. Perhaps some experiment by humans. I never took Highway 60 again.

*   *   *

Many years later, when I was an inspector on the Strategic Air Command (SAC) Inspector General Team, a B-52 pilot brazenly asked me, "What qualification do you have to inspect my crew?" I told him, for the benefit of the copilot also, "I have an ability to read. Your technical data says you will have an eye patch; I notice you don't have yours. Where is it?"

It turned out that his buddy had borrowed—and failed to return—his wartime eye patch so that he would look cool at a party thrown by one of the locals. Perhaps he didn't understand that under certain conditions, he would be required to wear the eye patch to protect at least his right eye in the event of encountering, close to his target, a nuclear flash from one of our ICBMs.

* * *

Over nearly two decades in the US Air Force, I had attended many of the regular, mandatory commander's call meetings. Typically these would be held monthly, in a base facility for group gatherings of about one hundred attendees—for example, every fourth Tuesday at 1100 hours. At F. E. Warren AFB in Wyoming, I was in command of a squadron myself—the 90 OMMS—and it was time for the scheduled commander's call.

I briskly walked into my first commander's call as a commander. The whole squadron seemed to be present, and they saw me enter. The informal conversations continued, so I had to call the outfit to attention in order to continue. Then I instructed, "This is how we are going to do this from now on. The first one to see me enter the room calls the rest of the squadron to attention." In front of their stunned silence, I turned, left the room, and came back in. They had gotten the message; someone called everyone to attention.

I stopped at the podium and inquired, "Are there any hot subjects that I need to cover?" There were none. I then announced, "I don't have any hot subjects either; you are dismissed." And with that I left the room. The whole event lasted less than fifteen minutes. At all future calls, they always came to attention as soon as I walked into the room. There were many important subjects to be covered at those following meetings.

Walking back to my office, I couldn't help but remember one of the very first impressions of a commander's call I attended when I reported to Vandenberg AFB, California. There was a new squadron commander by the name of Colonel Tre, and one of our attractive secretaries had walked about five blocks to the meeting. Two enlisted men, following behind, carried a large blackboard. The colonel moved up to the front of the room, and the group of about fifty quieted down. Then he spoke up and announced, "My name is Tre." Lovely Margo traipsed up to the front of the group, walked to the blackboard, and picked up a piece of chalk. The commander said, "My name is pronounced like 'tree.'" Margo wrote "Tre" on the blackboard. "Now I will turn you over to the technicians, who will show you an important movie." (It was a promotion for the sale of Series E bonds, as I remember—and the movie was long and boring.) He then walked out to return to his office. He must have spent two minutes talking to us. Margo and the two blackboard guys didn't watch the movie; they also left immediately, with their boss.

War Story Number Five

I was assigned to the 4315 Combat Crew Training Squadron at Vandenberg AFB when I heard Major H. relate this story.

Years earlier, as a lieutenant, he was stationed in New Delhi, India, flying the CBI (China, Burma, and India) theater operations. One time he had a mission to fly a Curtiss-Wright C-46 Commando as first pilot, to return a load of Chinese troops over the Hump, back to China. He looked back at the number of soldiers jammed into the cargo hold and observed loudly, "We'll never make it over the mountains unless we get rid of some weight."

Someone responded, "No problem!"

After takeoff, Lt. H. looked back to see his passengers were playing a serious game of paper, scissors, rock. After each round, the whole contingent would toss the loser out of the plane without a parachute. About a half dozen men had soon been tossed out of the open door by their companions, and the pilot figured the plane was probably light enough to get over the Hump. "That is enough!" he yelled. They closed the doors and sat silently for the rest of the trip. He never got over the fact that the group placed no value at all on human life; they were on a one-way trip, one way or another!

Military Career Awards

I've earned thirteen military medals, including the Bronze Star, Meritorious Service Medals (six), the Air Force Commendation Medal, the Combat Readiness Medal, the Vietnam Honor Medal, and the Vietnam Service

Medal for valor, service, and achievements. My Bronze Star was presented in spring 1974 for work on the Phoenix Program in the Vietnam War, during a PCS assignment in 1971.

*   *   *

Over the years of my career in the military, I also received other types of recognition, some related to extracurricular activities:

- **Highest Alert Rate**—1981, 1982, 1983 FE Warren AFB, Wyoming 90 OMMS shield, Missile Badge, Lt. Col. rank, SAC shield, commander brass plaque

- **Tour of Duty Presentation Plaque**—1981, Vandenberg AFB, California 3901 Strategic Missile Evaluation Squadron

- **Best Task Force Commander Presentation Plaque**—1983, FE Warren AFB, Wyoming 90 Strategic Missile Wing (SAC) (This was a recognition for exceptional innovations we had brought from Wyoming to our host in California, such as participation as a visiting flight of US Air Force officers and enlisted men during a flag-lowering ceremony. Also, we held an informal dining-in at the officer's club with guest of honor / speaker Major General Jack L. Watkins.)

- **Outstanding Maintenance Training Support Presentation Plaque**—1984, FE Warren 90 Strategic Missile Wing (SAC)

- **Commander's Presentation Plaque**—1984, FE Warren AFB, Wyoming 90 OMMS; presented on retirement

- **Photography**—1972, Malmstrom AFB, Montana. First place ribbon for outdoor photograph *Ant on Dandelion*

- **Racquetball**—1980, Vandenberg AFB, California Doubles racquetball base champions with partner Captain James Pruitt

I am also a life member of several military associations: the Air Force Association, the Air Commando Association (ACA), and the Retired Officer (TROA) / Military Officers of America (MOAA).

*   *   *

As a young officer at Vandenberg AFB, California, I used to listen to Captain Jim Sparks talk of significant events in his career; I called them war stories even then. Enraptured, I listened intently to each one. There's not much I can explain now—but I'll never forget him, his stories, and the positive influence he had on my development as a young officer. Jim was a captain at the time I knew him, and I was a first lieutenant. We were both ICBM crew procedures instructors assigned to the staff of the 4315th Combat Crew Training Squadron at Vandenberg Air Force Base. We taught ICBM combat crew procedures to every crewmember assigned to air force bases in the northern tier of the United States. This area was a huge geographic crescent that covered several states of the United States that we sarcastically but with fondness called the Banana Belt, mostly because of weather extremes—hot summers and very cold winters. In this book, I intend to carry forward his memory in the form of one of his war stories.

Jim Sparks was founder of the very first community service organization on a US Air Force base. From this organization at Vandenberg AFB came Project Handclasp, a suborganization that was our vehicle from which to launch several charitable programs to help local needy families.

One of our squadron's Needy Family Campaign efforts comes to mind. It was Christmastime, and we were to deliver several toys, plus a few snacks, to needy family groups. Jim was designated Santa Claus, and I his reindeer. In other words, I had promised not to drink any alcohol wherever we went. Jim, on the other hand, was Santa—and Santa could take a drink wherever and whenever he wished.

All this was part of the holiday season. And his reindeer could safely maneuver the car wherever Santa directed. It was also Santa's job to see that his reindeer was occupied and sober as the evening wore on, and as is often said of a successful operation, we were making good time on deliveries of our holiday season packages. Jim would ho-ho into a home in which we had already identified the exact number of children, while I would stay in the car. Of course the family would be expecting the arrival of Santa Claus, who was then greeted at the door with a tumbler of peppermint schnapps. As Santa, Jim would, of course, accept the gift. (As his reindeer, I, of course, would decline and continue to abstain.)

Then Jim would come back to our car, which was always wisely and mysteriously hidden out of sight in the dark, behind a tree or the corner of a house. He would greet his reindeer, settle in while fastening his seat belt in the process, and reach under the passenger seat for his bottle of his favorite bourbon. After he and I would share a laugh and a comment or two, Jim would take a hearty swig and then state with an authority borne of years of experience, "Next!" Then the reindeer would carefully drive to the next home.

The evening wore on, and at the very last home, he announced to the greeting family that he would "take two of those," waving his arm at the drink he had been offered at the front door. Of course, they had known Santa would visit that evening.

When our visit schedule was done, he dusted his hands and, with a "Ho ho ho" and a chuckle, started what he called "serious drinking." He reached under the car seat for the bottle and stated just before taking a healthy swallow, "There, that'll take care of the little bastards for one more year!" He gleefully laughed. Yet I could see right through him, because he just wasn't cynical. He loved this job and little kids so much. I chuckled with him and then drove us to our respective homes.

In late spring 2012, I sent a letter to Jim and Ruth Sparks in New Jersey, hoping I would catch him once more in one of his usual happy moods. I had not seen either of them for several years. I mentioned in my letter that I was writing a book of recollections and had found room in my book for one of his stories. Ruth quickly responded, "I am sorry to say that my Jim has passed away. He loved his military career so much, and wrote several books based on his experiences." Thanks, Jim. I couldn't have finished my career without you.

Chapter 5

In Between: Country Comes First

Cecil—A Family Cat from Indiana

What is a cat named Cecil without a little background to go along with the name? You ought to read this if you want to find out how a cat lives its life without eyeballs. You read that right—without eyeballs! I worked for the Erie Railroad during that first summer after high school graduation. One hot July day, right after I had experienced a recurrence of malaria chills, a bedraggled grayish cat came up to me and meowed pitifully. I was surprised, but I immediately befriended it and put it in the left pocket of my old US Army jacket I had worn that morning. It just cuddled up in my suffocatingly hot pocket and went to sleep. I was still suffering from the malaria chills and was wearing the coat despite the hot temperature. I named my new friend Erie Cat and took it home at the end of the day. In the fall, I started college at Purdue University, about seventy-five miles away, and I left Erie Cat at home with the barn cats. Before winter she bore a litter of six kittens; two were stillborn, two had disfigured limbs, one had no eyeballs, and only one seemed to be normal. Our Oliver family realized that the caring mother cat must have been affected by creosote or other railroad chemicals.

As the kittens continued to grow, my mama and papa were good caregivers, and they fed the neglected members of the litter with an eyedropper when Erie Cat would permit only the normal kitten to have access to her milk. I was in touch with them, and when I heard about the litter, I started to feel guilty for interfering with Mother Nature by befriending and picking up Erie Cat. The disabled kittens would not have survived if they had been left on their own. One day Papa asked me over the phone, "What shall Mama and I do with the blind kitten?" I mentioned to him I would come by and pick it up and care for it myself. (By this time, I was married to Joye and we had an off-campus apartment near Purdue University, where we could keep the kitten safely.)

After we picked up the young cat from the farm and were living with it in Lafayette, Indiana, we took it to a veterinarian for a checkup. He volunteered that he could put medicated cotton inside the eye sockets and sew the eyelids shut to prevent inevitable infection, at no cost to a struggling university student. We named the cat Cecilia, which I learned was a German name meaning "blind virgin." In the meantime, Joye and I were so poor that we shared a toy stuffed alligator that we gave back and forth to each other as a humorous exchange of gifts. (Wrapping and unwrapping it and wrapping it again on subsequent occasions didn't bother us, because we always knew things would get better tomorrow.)

One day I found Cecilia making obvious masculine advances involving the stuffed toy alligator, and Joye and I immediately changed the cat's name to Cecil. The name change didn't make a difference to the animal's uncanny ability to make its way around the apartment. Visitors would come and go, never realizing there was anything wrong with our cat. One day a friend of mine finally made a comment about Cecil. He said, "There is something about that cat; I think that cat is squinting at us!" I didn't have the heart to tell him that his eyes were sewn shut.

One day Joye and I brought Cecil's healthy brother from the farm to our apartment to visit Cecil for a week so he could be around a normal cat. Big mistake. A cat born without eyes to see has no idea what daylight is and does not know when it is nighttime. So at midnight, he and his brother were romping around, which kept us from getting any sleep. Joye went around with a flyswatter the entire next day, poking the cats to keep them from taking a nap. The very next weekend, we returned the brother cat back to the farm.

Cecil continued to amaze us with his sightless antics. For example, he would run clear across the room, jump up on the bed, and swat a fly crawling on the window screen—he would nail the fly every time! We did notice that his whiskers were very long, and his hearing was exceptional as well. One time my wife and I put him on top of the refrigerator. With no hesitation, Cecil knew he was at an increased height and meowed pitifully. After he studied the situation a little bit longer, he confidently jumped down to the seat of a nearby chair; and from the chair, he jumped once more—to the floor this time. We humans looked at each other in amazement. Not bad for a cat with no eyes and no visual concept of differing heights!

Cecil traveled with us in the car from the Purdue campus to Gary, Indiana, and then on to Marianna, Florida—my first military assignment. A year later, in the early 1960s, we all traveled again to Reese AFB, adjacent to Lubbock, Texas. Here Cecil achieved some notoriety when a reporter from the Lubbock *Avalanche-Journal* newspaper heard of him somehow and stopped by for a visit with such an usual cat. The result was a detailed story of a family living with a sightless cat, complete with photographs. In a few months, Cecil joined us as our family moved on to Vandenberg AFB in California, where I began a career with ICBMs.

After several years of living a totally housecat existence, Cecil somehow got outside our California home and was lost. I was looking and calling for Cecil all over the area. I hiked and discovered parts of Vandenberg AFB that I didn't know even existed. I hiked and hiked. I finally found him in a nearby lake, where he had been thrown to drown—totally helpless with no ability to see, let alone swim. Cecil had probably been picked up by a community security guard who was diligently enforcing the "no unattended pets" rule. Besides, Cecil had no inspection or ID tags— because he was indoors with us all the time. Anyway, it was a very sad end of an era for me and my special feline friend, Cecil.

*   *   *

I married an engineering student named Joye in my junior year at Purdue University. We divorced five years later, sharing three children: Laura, now in Denver, Colorado; Karin, with a master's degree, and her family in North Carolina; and corporate private pilot and retired US Army Black Hawk helicopter instructor/pilot, as well as Sherpa straight-wing instructor/pilot, James, in Louisiana. I vowed never to marry again, but after five years, I met a teacher in Rapid City, South Dakota, who looked so much like a Hollywood starlet I married her. After five more years and a son, Michael, we divorced during readjustments that I failed to successfully complete on my return from the Vietnam War. About this time I adopted a philosophy of five-year fear regarding marital relationships.

The custody arrangement with my first three children allowed me to have them during the summer months, wherever I was stationed. I would drive to pick them up and make arrangements for family housing off-base in the nearby local city. For three months of many years, I willingly juggled military duties with the responsibilities of a single father. I cherished the opportunity to be a real part of their lives, no matter how demanding it may have felt at the time.

Highway 66 Reflections

After making up my mind that I would visit the kids, who were living with their mother in Lubbock, Texas, I took California Highway 101 southward from Vandenberg AFB, in California to Los Angeles. I traveled Highway 66 a total of thirteen times in a two-year period to visit my three kids. I would pick up Highway 66 somewhere in Los Angeles and then head eastward.

I will always remember my initial stopover at Needles, California. I had decided to check into a motel and restart my eastward trip when the weather cooled off. However, the temperature was still ninety-nine degrees at midnight when I restarted.

I was young and crazy. At a point during nighttime driving on one of my thirteen trips, I had to stop the car in order to determine what was wrong with it. I thought the turn signal was on because I was seeing a flashing light. Upon stopping, I realized the light I had seen was just the white center line passing by outside the car window. My perception was all screwed up. I had white-line fever from driving too long.

On Highway 66, the state police hid behind billboards. I had heard that the cops would pull over and ticket anyone who was driving in the opposite direction who warned oncoming traffic of their presence by flashing their headlights.

This is where my decision to return to Vandenberg by way of Highway 60 on one of my trips gains some significance. Two highways paralleled each other from Amarillo, Texas, to Snowflake, Arizona. The same night that I took Highway 60 westbound, a guy named Mad Dog Irvin was killing people on Highway 66. He was shooting through the glass of car windows as he drove and at rest stops. The police were in a tizzy trying to catch him, and they finally caught up with him in Los Angeles!

In the early morning hours, my only companion was the car radio playing, loud and clear, XELO from Juarez, Mexico. The music was lively and the DJs clever, and the combination helped keep me awake.

*   *   *

The young kids that lived with me during the summer months have grown up and have families of their own. My son James Reece Oliver, his sweet wife, Julie Ann, and their beautiful children (my grandkids) have all brought me overwhelming joy—little Reece Alexis, James Castile (the only relative I know who carries the name of a city as his middle name), and young Marshall Haden. We often mail them cookies that have been mixed and baked in a bakery a block away.

Having pretty much the same name as your son causes things to get mixed up sometimes. One time I was calling from my home phone in Denver, Colorado, to my son Jim at his workplace, in Wichita, Kansas. After a few rings, there was an answer, and I stated, "Hello, this is Jim Oliver."

I got an immediate response before I could ask to speak to my son, Jim: "Hey, Jim, what in the heck are you doing in Denver?" It took a little explaining to straighten out the confusion.

Daughter Karin Lee Cox and her sweet kids (again, also my grandkids) Austin Robert Hartsook, Rachel June Cox, and Keith Douglas Cox have brought me great pleasure watching them grow into such talented and interesting adults. Karin is special in my life because whatever she attempted to do, she achieved and then completed. In this regard, she aimed for and earned a master's degree in fine arts from Wichita State University in Kansas. She is now vice president of a nonprofit corporation and has recently assumed duties as chief creative officer of the corporation.

Distant, but also my first child, is my daughter Laura Ann Oliver, who has renamed herself Lara. She contributed to development of my book by taking the time to assume the responsibility of welcoming long-lost Oliver cousins during the 2011 Oliver Cousins Reunion held in Denver,

Colorado. She also provided wonderful notebooks for everyone containing Oliver family history, photographs, and genealogy. Unfortunately, I have completely lost touch with my youngest son, Michael Robert Oliver.

Mixing a Gator Ball

When my partner and I won the Malmstrom AFB handball championship competition, we qualified to go to an annual tournament at Barksdale AFB, in Louisiana. We flew on a courier plane that made round trips regularly between the two bases, transporting classified "go-codes" for the military bombers and missiles. My partner and I won the first game 21 to 2 against the representatives from Lowry Air Training Base in Denver; we taught them a thing or two about handball! The next day, we played another SAC base from Pease AFB, in New Hampshire. The two guys from Pease taught us a thing or two about the game! Our first game began first thing in the morning, and by 10:00, we were defeated.

When you are defeated so badly, it is always your partner's fault because you played your side better than he did. After the games, local reporters came up to us and asked all sorts of questions. I recall that one asked me, "To what do attribute your defeat?"

I quickly replied, "My partner—he just learned the game a half hour before the tournament."

The very same reporter asked my partner, "To what do attribute your defeat?"

He said, "My partner—he just learned the game a half hour before the tournament." I just have to guess that we were closer partners than the guys from some SAC base who won the tourney.

On the way out of the gym, my partner grabbed a bottle of Gatorade off a hospitality table that had been set up for participants from the various bases. We headed back to our housing. On our way past the officers' club, I picked up a bottle of Black Label Jack Daniel's—an excellent whiskey.

By that time, the rancor had left me, and I told my partner, "I'm going to teach you how to mix a gator ball; it's as simple as falling off a log!" (Of course I didn't tell him that is exactly what my high school classmates used to tell me while I was in high school in northern Indiana!) "Fifty-fifty, Gatorade plus whiskey." Of course I also didn't tell him that the Gatorade took the whiskey quickly to the veins and arteries of the body. I do not need to add that we were snockered before lunchtime—which began at eleven thirty.

Exploring at Pactola Reservoir

In the spring of 1968, soon after my PCS military reassignment from Vandenberg Air Force Base, in California, to Ellsworth Air Force Base, in South Dakota, I was on a hike to explore Black Hills National Forest, in South Dakota. I was near the entrance of a small-time prospector's mine, just west of Pactola Reservoir, which is west of Rapid City. That's where I discovered a weathered heap of rail spikes, much smaller in overall dimension than the spikes used by a narrow-gauge railroad maintenance crew. Ever since living in the railroad country of Akron, Indiana, I have been fascinated with trains of all types. Finding these tiny spikes set my imagination into high gear. I assumed they must have been used on tracks hauling ore out of a nearby mining operation.

I had recently run across larger railroad spikes for sale in a souvenir shop. It seemed to me that there would be an even greater demand for this smaller version, especially for executives thinking about the next great idea. I could just see a New York City executive of some large corporation doing some serious thinking while he touched these diminutive spikes from somewhere out West. He would pick one up, rub his thumb across the smooth edge, and think about getting out of the big city for a while.

Anyway, one of the advantages of getting out on an excursion such as this was that I could let my mind wander and wonder, away from the usual duties and responsibilities of my day-to-day life in the military.

Continuing Education

Learning about the world we live in has been important to me from the time I was a small child. After I graduated from Purdue University and embarked on my career in the air force, there was always more to learn, and I did my best to keep up with it. My additional concentrated efforts in the formal education arena are:

- 1964 (three months temporary duty)—Attended Squadron Officer School at Maxwell AFB, Air University, Montgomery, Alabama

- 1967—Enrolled in and completed graduate courses in economics available through an Air Force Institute of Technology extension program offered with South Dakota State University

- 1970 September to December—US Army schooling at the John Fitzgerald Kennedy United States Army Institute for Military Assistance (JFKUSAIMA), Fort Bragg, North Carolina, where I completed the Unit Psychological Operations Officer Course

- 1976—Graduate of USAF seminars at Industrial College of the Armed Forces and Air Command and Staff College

- 1977—Between SAC duties and after work at night, took graduate courses in international relations at Creighton University in Omaha, Nebraska

- 1981—Earned a master's degree in public administration from Golden Gate University, in California, where I was also a member of the 400 Club (a regional recognition association for students who earn A grades in all courses of a graduate program, sponsored by Golden Gate University)

- 1981—Graduate of USAF seminars: at Air War College and Industrial College of the Armed Forces

Cold Turkey I

Quitting smoking wasn't easy. I went from smoking my favorite Camel cigarettes—short, unfiltered cigarette-paper-and-cut-tobacco cigarettes—to not being dependent on smoking at all. The last time I had an urge to smoke was in 1966, when I quit cold turkey. Doctors have since told me that anything alien to good health that is willfully ingested into one's body is generally an excellent candidate for causing cancer. In my view, cigarettes are not an exception. I wanted to quit smoking. I term it "cold turkey I" because I did it again to control my drinking.

This is how it worked for me:

1. Decide you really want to quit smoking.
    (a) Smoke as usual, whenever you need to do it.
    (b) Set a definite date when you will begin your quit-smoking program.
    (c) Define a plan of action: break up the ultimate objective into achievable pieces.
    (d) Open a fresh pack of cigarettes and keep them within easy reach in your left breast pocket.
    (e) Do not smoke for one whole day.

2. As you reach each step, give yourself credit! Don't forget to pat yourself on the back!
    (a) Congratulate yourself after each day of your program to quit smoking.
    (b) After a week, you will know that you have achieved a milestone just by smelling flowers and things that you knew had an odor to them though you did not give yourself a chance to smell them! You will just feel healthier too. And you will walk around beaming, and people about you will never know why you are so lighthearted. Of course you do not want to tell them of your achievement, simply because you have so much more time left in your program to quit. Tobacco addiction, after all, is a dependence situation. It is not simply a habit that you are trying to break; it is a deeply established dependence on the addictive substance.

After about thirty days of carrying around a trashy pack of crumbling cigarettes that were messing up my jacket pocket, I proudly threw them away. That was that. I quit, and I haven't had (or wanted) a single cigarette since!

*   *   *

Mike and Veryl McBride live just two floors below my wife and me and have been good friends since we all moved into the newly renovated condominium complex in 1995. They never forget us on a holiday with a note, card, or doorknob surprise. Now, in recent times, we enjoy the digital wonders of an animated e-card, in full color and accompanied with lovely music. They are always thinking of others and helping any way they can. For me they represent the sincere friendship that makes life a whole lot more special.

When Mike was sent overseas on a military assignment during the Vietnam War, his little girl Laura Jean was just a few years old. His wife, Veryl, aware that the little one was growing up very quickly, kept the nice photograph of Mike prominently displayed where they could regularly say hello and remember that even though he was far away, he was still part of their family.

On returning home, Mike showed up at the door, and Veryl announced with great excitement, "Here's Daddy!" After standing there for a moment in a state of confusion and disbelief, little Laura Jean ran into the bedroom and returned with their family photograph of Mike. Pointing to the daddy that she knew in the 8" × 10" photo frame, with a sense of determined loyalty, she proclaimed to all present, "No, that's Daddy!"

Chapter 6

The Vietnam War: We Are the Enemy

Special Operations

From Strategic Air Command (SAC) missile combat crew commander duties in South Dakota, I was sent to the school at John Fitzgerald Kennedy United States Army Institute for Military Assistance (JFKUSAIMA— which I contend must be the longest string of abbreviations used in the US military establishment) at Ft. Bragg, North Carolina, for training in US Army special operations. Then, in January 1971, I was assigned to Vietnam to join a mixed civilian-military team, Advisory Team 43 of the Military Assistance Command–Vietnam (abbreviated to MACV, which locally was pronounced "mac-vee"). After a year in a combat zone in Vietnam, I was reassigned to ICBMs as a maintenance officer in Montana,

From August 1970 through December, I received training with the US Army at Fort Bragg as a psychological warfare advisor. There were ninety-six officers in our class: six US Air Force officers (including me), about ten officers of the Royal Thai Army, a major from the Philippine Army, five officers of the People's Army of Vietnam, a captain in the Mexican Army, a captain from Iran, and a major equivalent (termed a deputy squadron leader) of the Australian Army. The rest of the class consisted of junior-ranked officers of the US Army. It was generally understood and expected that soon after graduation, every member of the class would be sent to the Vietnam War. One of my classmates, the major from the Philippines, eventually became a congressman, and later, chief of the Defense Department of the Philippines.

Training time in the Fort Bragg environment went beyond the classroom and included picking up on such attitude-changers as the well-known motto of special operations, a paraphrased version of a psalm: "Yea, though I walk through the valley of the shadow of Death, I shall fear no Evil—for I am the meanest SOB in this here valley!"

We usually spent off-duty time at the officers' club, where a lot of women congregated. Ft. Bragg, North Carolina, was where five thousand widows settled in because they just couldn't get the US Army out of their systems. They couldn't think of going back to the cornfields of Iowa, Ohio, or Indiana, and life in general was not to their liking. Most of their negative motivation came from Mom and Dad, and usually in the form of disapproval of their lives so far: "Welcome back to the mom and dad you spurned when you married that dude—what's his name?—and now he's dead."

I took advantage of extracurricular skydiving. It was my attempt to cure acrophobia, and it turned out badly. My intentions were clear, and I diligently listened and practiced during the on-the-ground training session. When the time for jumping arrived, I actually packed my chute and boarded the small plane with no door on it. We flew up, and up, and up. When we were over the landing area, the instructor yelled, "Jump!"

I froze physically, but mentally I knew a demanding order when I heard one, and I stepped out of that nice secure airplane with a floor. Immediately I had second thoughts, and my hands were scrambling frantically to grab onto the struts of the airplane that was moving rapidly away from me. A basic instinct for survival took over, and I pulled the cord to open that wonderful chute, ready and waiting to do its job. What followed was a period of elation, which was a far cry from the fearful panic I had experienced only moments before. In due time, I landed as I had been taught, with no difficulty or apprehension. I was never so glad to be back on terra firma!

The jump instructor had a few angry words for me: "What were you doing grabbing for the plane? Your chute could have gotten tangled, causing the plane to crash and killing us all!" He had nothing to worry about, since I would never jump out of a plane like that again in my lifetime. So much for the expenditure of $26.84 to learn skydiving to cure a fear of heights!

I still deal with acrophobia. It continues to be a challenge because I like to take photos and watch fireworks from the thirty-ninth-floor balconies of our home in downtown Denver. At least now I am sure that what I thought would be a skydiving cure is much worse than the fear of being up high!

A SOSA and Vietnamization

Anyone who would have tried to follow my movements when I was assigned to the Vietnam War would have been bamboozled! Early in January 1971, after completing the Training Course in Special Operations at Ft. Bragg, I traveled alone to Vietnam. Leaving from Ellsworth, my home base, I flew to Travis AFB, in California, and then boarded one of the many military transport flights leaving daily to Vietnam. Upon arrival in Saigon, I reported to an administrative office as instructed, where all my papers and identification documents were changed and I was reassigned to the US Embassy. In a couple of days, my papers were changed again (in an effort to not leave a paper trail for anyone to follow), and I was sent in-country to Hau Nghia Province.

For the next eleven months, I was assigned to the Joint United States Public Affairs Office, a major adjunct of the United States Information Service during the Vietnam War. I was a thirty-four-year-old US Air Force major when I went to Vietnam as a special operations staff advisor (SOSA) with air force specialty code 2111. This was an entry-level AFSC; in six months it would be changed to 2116 to indicate that with the passage of the required time on the job in the same AFSC, I was fully qualified.

During the Vietnam War in the late 1960s, MACV established a "country team," actually an advisory team, in each of the provinces of South Vietnam. I joined about 275 other warfare specialists on the team, including members of the Central Intelligence Agency (CIA); the United States Information Agency (USIA)—my parent organization, which had a long-standing reputation of never being involved in combat operations; the US Agency for International Development (USAID), which, like USIA, was also reputed to never be involved in combat operations; and US Army combat troops. The US Army was tasked mostly with intelligence-gathering and training missions. A few US Army Special Forces members were also on the team. I was the sole US Air Force member, and I reported to the Joint US Public Affairs Office, a subordinate organization of the USIA. I wore civilian clothes and carried an M16 rifle wherever I went.

An advisory team was under a US Army commander tasked with transferring war-waging functions from US forces to South Vietnamese commanders and their soldiers during the "Vietnamization" phase of a war that had dragged on far too long. The USA was intent on extricating itself, one way or another, from continued involvement in this protracted conflict, which had already cost our country close to fifty-eight thousand soldiers, not to mention the huge amount of money involved or the anguish associated with every conflict.

The war was already thirteen years old when I arrived in January 1971. I was assigned to MACV Advisory Team 43 in Hau Nghia Province, which was reputed by multiple-assignment old-timer-soldiers to be "the most active and hottest piece of real estate in all Vietnam, between the Ho Chi Minh Trail and Saigon."

At the time, Saigon was the capital city of South Vietnam. The Ho Chi Minh Trail was the major weapon-supply road that paralleled the entire length of South Vietnam, but it was located "on the other side"—in Laos and Cambodia, supposedly neutral countries that bordered South Vietnam. Four years later, North Vietnam and local Vietcong forces overwhelmed the southern army and, within mere days, among other objectives, renamed the capital of South Vietnam as Ho Chi Minh City.

By most accounts, I was already an old man—a senior citizen in this "young man's war"—simply because I was thirty-four years old. A major at the time, I was the province psychological warfare advisor for Hau Nghia Province. As PPA, my job was to support the Phoenix effort, a US program that focused on identification and neutralization of Vietcong infrastructure (VCI)—individuals who were key to the enemy's "shadow government." As PPA, my tasks primarily addressed the process of neutralization of VCI members. Within that area of responsibility, implementing an approach of convincing VCI individuals to abandon their political and military inclinations was of the greatest importance on my daily list of things to do. Thus, I became a participant in several singularly unconventional events.

No Greater Love—Ba Chiem

The process of identification was mostly the bailiwick of district intelligence operations centers, with any relevant input expected of the PPA. A factual input was whatever we could corroborate with some evidence.

One particularly important, not to mention dangerous, member of the VCI was Tu Chiem, a hard-core Communist who had come up through the ranks, both political and military. He had been fighting in wars since his youth—under the leadership of General Ho Chi Minh in the late 1930s, to recent atrocities in 1971. He had used force against French colonialists, the Japanese invaders during WWII, and then the French once more at Dien Bien Phu, before concentrating on killing American soldiers starting in the early 1960s. About sixty years old, he had spent fully thirty-five of those years firing a gun in one war or another. He was a dedicated professional, rumored an efficient killer, and certainly an expert battle organizer.

Given Tu Chiem's reputation, we had to take him down. In early March 1971, we began an intensive search throughout the province. He was elusive, however, and uncannily avoided several ambushes we had set up. No-notice drop-in searches were also fruitless. The team's combat patrols often stopped at his house, which was a little, run-down thatched hut with a mud floor, where his frail wife, Ba Chiem, lived. She was tiny and emaciated; her health was not good. What few teeth she had left were discolored from years of chewing betel nut. On several previous visits, we had given her aspirin tablets and other simple medicines. She was not our enemy; we didn't have a conflict with her. It was her husband, the dedicated revolutionary and planner, we wanted. Yet, whenever we inquired of his whereabouts, her answer was the same: "He is gone. He went north to visit relatives. He will be away many months."

"Going north" meant to North Vietnam, home to many relatives of the South Vietnamese. We didn't believe her, though, and continued our province-wide dragnet for the next several months. Interestingly enough, attacks on our outposts had decreased somewhat, so we thought maybe he really had left the area for a while.

After half a year of searching (of course with the help of observers in helicopters), setting up ambushes in the stifling humidity of dark nights alive with stinging insects of all sorts, looking far and wide from house to house, and employing our soldiers to tediously sweep the dangerous swamp in the heat of many relentless suns, we failed to find Tu Chiem. Then one day someone noticed a worn path that went nowhere. It stretched from Tu Chiem's thatched hut to a mound of earth close to a banyan tree, and that was it. The troops picked up entrenching tools, and amid surprising and inexplicable wails and protests from the tiny woman, they dug into the mound. There they soon uncovered a body wrapped in a US Army poncho (which is actually a ubiquitous item where military activities prevail).

As we observed the exhumation, a horde of flies immediately appeared around us. Despite the advanced decomposition of the body, our intelligence specialists identified the ring on the right hand as belonging to Tu Chiem. Also, the well-known scar on the decayed flesh of his left cheek was still visible, and of course the carcass was loosely draped in the dark blue nylon uniform in which he had been buried.

The uniform of the North Vietnamese Army was usually carried in a small backpack. These uniforms were also issued to Vietcong citizen-soldiers along with verbal orders to don them and mass the force plus the firepower of a regular army—only when the time was right. (In 1975, they donned them on a vocal order.)

With Tu Chiem's wife wailing softly in the background, we reburied his body. Someone commented, "This guy's been dead for months."

We motioned the interpreter toward the dead soldier's wife, Ba Chiem, and instructed, "Ask her what happened to him. Why didn't she tell us he was dead? Tell her we won't harm her, but we do need some answers." Little by little, the interpreter was able to momentarily calm the distraught woman. During a short conversation, she conveyed an astounding story:

"My husband died long ago, in the middle of March, while crossing the swamp with members of his cadre, when he was struck by fragments of artillery. I buried him next to the tree. Throughout our life together, I never understood his politics, and I didn't know what he did, but it must have been very important, because you kept looking for him. I loved him, and that is why I never told you he was dead. I knew you would spend much time and money continuing to search for him. It was the least I could do in memory of my beloved husband."

I have seen many things, but never have I seen a greater expression of love than Ba Chiem demonstrated, for indeed we had spent thousands of man-hours and immeasurable resources in search of a ghost! Finally released from her self-imposed vow of silence, she cried uncontrollably, her heartrending wails circumscribing the depth of her pent-up grief. For six months she had denied herself an opportunity to grieve for him. Now her bereavement was intense. She let open the floodgates of emotion.

Our troops dispersed. Hours later, heading back to our team compound in the gathering dusk, I drove my jeep past the thatched hut. Ba Chiem was still on her knees next to the mound of dirt, her tiny shoulders shaking. I thought that although she was a simple country woman who knew nothing of war, or what her husband did, or the reasons men fight other men for thirty-five years straight, the depth of her intense love and total dedication to a dead husband foretold the difficult time we would have winning this war.

Vietnam Vignettes

To check out some new information about the VCI activities that our office had received, I scheduled a nonemergency helicopter for transportation. The chopper did not show up as scheduled, and I was furious to be left just standing around and waiting when there was so much work waiting to be addressed! Then I felt remorse and sadness when I received an explanation of what had caused the unexpected delay.

A young lieutenant had been killed in action somewhere in the field. His body was being sent home ceremoniously and with great care. Then his missing arm was finally found and wrapped in dry ice, and my requested helicopter was redirected. The new duty assignment was to quickly catch up and deliver the severed arm of the young soldier's body on its way back to the United States and a grieving family.

* * *

I was collecting pieces of shrapnel as a thirty-four-year-old USAF major during the Vietnam War after a night of shelling by the North Vietnamese Army, who launched 122mm rockets at our team headquarters in Bao Trai. I was just using the activity as a mindless diversion during a few quiet moments, when I suddenly realized I had done this before, as a child—almost thirty years earlier, during the terrors of WWII in the Philippines. Here I was, in Vietnam, approximately one thousand miles to the west, at practically the same latitude, and I was once again searching out the sharp-edged shards, just as my brother Bob and I did as kids when we were hiding in Kawá-Kawá on the Philippine island of Mindanao. In both cases, I used an oval-shaped sardine can to collect the metal pieces! Now, as an adult, I know that no one is a winner in this game—it would be better to have no shrapnel to pick up from the tortured ground of wartime.

*   *   *

In Vietnam, I ran into another version of the natural horrors that I experienced as a child in the Philippines (such as the centipede devouring the little vole). I observed a large spider with a black-and-yellow trapezoid-shaped body that spun a web of very sticky yellow filament that trapped and caught a bird. As the bird attempted to free itself, the spider simply detected activity in its web and scampered across its web to the site. Next, it wrapped the victim with additional strands of sticky filament until it was nothing but prey wrapped in a ball of sticky webbing, glistening in the sun! That is, the spider probably stuck a proboscis of sorts through its own strands of filament, and, sight unseen, simply sucked the juices out of whatever it had caught in its web, leaving nothing but very dry feathers and bones that had once been a bird.

*   *   *

Walking around Hau Nghia Provence, where I worked daily in my search for VCI, I would meet families. Most of the young children had distended stomachs, which I have learned is usually a sign of protein deficiency. This severe deficiency is called kwashiorkor. These families did not have household pets, because goldfish and dogs and cats were excellent sources of protein. We had an assistant who ate swamp cockroaches, probably as a source of protein, and his name was Mopp. (For some reason, I always thought he was a double-agent Vietcong soldier, but that is neither here nor there.)

I personally observed the absence of any dogs or cats in Bao Tri. Then, after observing Mopp, who ate bugs, it became clear to me. The people needed protein. This was swamp country in Vietnam, and dogs and cats were literally fair game as food. Pets were a good source of protein.

*   *   *

I was awaiting an inbound helicopter carrying two VIPs when a rainstorm came through. Finally I heard the helicopter approaching. It was a light observation helicopter (LOH). I saw a lightning bolt hit a claymore mine, which had been placed as usual on a nearby fence post at the edge of our protected area. When it exploded, it released BBs in an outward direction for about fifty feet. The helicopter all of a sudden appeared from out of the rain clouds and landed with a thump. The pilot immediately bailed out of his seat, ran past me, and shouted, "Incoming! Incoming!" I recognized him as he ran past me; he was a combat veteran and should have known the difference between enemy fire and a claymore mine explosion. But I guess, as combat troops used to say in more peaceful times, one doesn't really contemplate his navel at times like this.

A Dire Prediction

One day during my early childhood years in the Philippines, our nanny Marciana took my small four-year-old right hand and intently studied the lines on my palm. She looked at me a very long time before making a pronouncement: "You will die a violent death just before you become thirty-five years old. I cannot see how you will die, but you will." I read a great deal of darkness and foreboding in the manner she told me about her prediction, so naturally, I conveyed my concerns to Mama. From that point on, Marciana was very distant from the child who tattled on her. Mama must have had a talk with her, and in my mind's eye, I imagined their confidential meeting was not a warm one.

The prediction didn't mean much to me at the time, because I was only a preschooler. I didn't know then what I would be doing when I came close to her doomsday age, but years later in Vietnam, when I was thirty-four years old, her words came back to haunt me. I was a major in the US Air Force by then, but her prediction came from out of nowhere and became one more worry on my back—and that new concern was whether I would survive my tour or become just another statistic of some lucky sniper. Although I spent the year productively and without serious incident, Marciana's prediction weighed heavily on my mind every day. I am now seventy-eight and have always felt I was living on borrowed time. I'm simply glad Marciana was wrong!

*   *   *

In December 1971, as I boarded my plane in Saigon International Airport, the air temperature and humidity were both approximately the same—about ninety-five degrees and ninety-five percent, respectively. The temperature was high enough to generate a heat-index warning, as I recollect. The troop plane had a stopover in Japan (Itazuke AB, I believe) for refueling or crew change. We passengers were allowed three hours or so to get off the plane, stretch our legs—whatever. I made my way to the base exchange and bought Little Ben, a pendulum wall clock that chimes on the hour in my home—a daily reminder of my gratitude for returning alive from the Vietnam War.

After a couple of days, the lengthy trip that began in the tropics of Vietnam finally ended with the last leg of flying, and I was dropped off in Rapid City, South Dakota. Temperatures were negative fifty-five, with a wind chill factor well below that. What a shock!

*   *   *

The Colclazier family had long-term positive effects on me both in my being a Vietnam vet trying to find himself again and in my military leadership roles. The group consisted of Robert (whom I affectionately called Colonel C. in recognition of a surname that my contemporaries found difficult to pronounce or even spell); his accomplished kids Ted, Sue, Linda, and Dale (two girls and two boys, as in the classic two-pair poker hand), and of course his sweet wife, Kay.

Many years ago, Colonel C. was commander of the 341st Minuteman Maintenance Squadron (341 MiMS) at Malmstrom AFB, in Montana. Within this squadron of many splendors, I was consecutively assigned as officer-in-charge of the 341 MiMS Field Maintenance Branch, Organizational Maintenance Branch, and a short time later, the Vehicle and Equipment Control Branch. Over a few years as officer-in-charge of the three Minuteman III ICBM major maintenance branches of the squadron, I garnered hands-on experience that did me well during my next military assignment as an ICBM maintenance inspector on the SAC Headquarters Inspector General Team, Offutt AFB, Nebraska.

On a follow-up assignment, Colonel C. became commander of Disaster Control and Management programs of US forces in Europe. Even after our individual retirements from military duty several years later, we corresponded. He was an excellent leader and military mentor to me. It was because of him that I started collecting memories for some future book. In retrospect, time has gone by so quickly that a once-distant future is *today*—that is, *right now!*

It was the entire Colclazier family who played a major role in normalizing me during post-Vietnam War adjustments, through demonstrating to me the interactions of members of a day-to-day family. At the time, I was secretly delighted in observing—and honored to be a part of—the decision-making processes of the entire family.

War Story Number Six

I heard this story from a captain who was with me in the 66 SMS, 44SMW, at Ellsworth AFB, in South Dakota. When I knew him first, he was a maintenance combat crew commander who was picked by Headquarters for a special assignment because he spoke fluent French. Much later, when he returned to Ellsworth, I tried to find out what the mystery mission had been all about. Finally, one evening at the officers' club, he explained some of the details.

He was officer-in-charge of the contingent that went to Bikini Atoll, where the United States had been doing extensive nuclear explosives testing. In those early years, nuclear explosives were inefficient, and some of our test bombs didn't work at all. Whole islands disappeared. Sometimes only partial nuclear reactions occurred, leaving large melted metal globs all over the ground. Only rats and cockroaches were thriving in the radioactive environment now; humans had been driven out, and the remaining living things had retreated back into their burrows to eventually die. In later years of testing, deliveries became more efficient, and results more precise.

Chapter 7

In Between: Tough Winters, Gentle Springs

From Military to Civilian Life

I retired from the Air Force in January 1984, and by the end of February I had moved to Denver, Colorado, and a new employment position with the Martin Marietta Corporation. The company was preparing proposals for government projects regarding various aspects of ICBM functionality and operations. (The MX ICBM was included.) My military experience and technical writing ability fit in with the need of proposal teams. The work was intense, and the teams of coworkers congenial; all in all, it worked out to be an interesting progression of work responsibilities and a productive transition into civilian life. My position titles and some of the programs I worked on are listed below:

- senior logistics engineer
  strategic systems, Peacekeeper-in-Minuteman-Silo (PIMS) Program
- senior logistics engineer
  space systems, integrated logistics analysis, Space Station Program
- principal investigator IR&D
  strategic systems, hard mobile launcher (for the Small ICBM)—1986
- representative, program logistics
  strategic systems, Rail Garrison Program (by this time, the MX Missile [ICBM] was called the Peacekeeper)

Honors and Recognition, Martin Marietta Denver Aerospace

- o Technical Achievement Award—1987
- o Outstanding IR&D Principal Investigators (12)—1986
- o Logistics Employee of the Month—July 1986

After retirement from the USAF in 1984, thus ending career number one, I hired into Martin Marietta Aerospace Corporation for career number two as a logistics representative. I then was laid off in 1991. When I look at the positive side of things, this latter event was propitious because it prepared me for career number three, by all accounts the most illustrious and enjoyable career of my three careers—my career as a part-time writer.

My wife, Louise, was chief executive officer, and I president, of our home-based company, Questers Advisory Group, Inc., which we formed in 1992. Its focus was on business analysis as well as literary and commercial writing. Her last consulting contract resulted in a permanent job with a large telecommunications company in downtown Denver, Colorado. She retired in 1997. Our little company compiled and edited teaching guides for the Head Start regional office in Phoenix, Arizona. We were tickled pink when we learned that some of the guides were being used at international locations. In addition, over a period of seven years, we wrote and published a monthly retirement-community newsletter for over three thousand readers. In a literary effort in 1997, we published our first book, *Grandpa's Very Short Stories*, ISBN 1-57502-635-X.

Nature

I am a naturalist at heart. I solo backpacked for at least forty-five years, mostly after returning from the Vietnam War, and loved every solitary moment of the locations I visited and the chance to be directly connected to the natural world at its best—and sometimes at its worst! When I was a child in the Philippines, I was continually amazed at the observations I could make in the world of nature. Over the years, in many different places and a wide variety of ways, I have continued to enjoy learning about the natural world. Almost any time I am outdoors in nature, there is a sight or a situation that I find amazing to behold and to think about. I'll share a just a few examples in this section to explain what I mean.

A flying squirrel, the first I'd ever seen, was in the Bob Marshall Wilderness, west of Augusta, Montana. I was hiking slowly along the trail with my heavily loaded backpack in September 1972 when the squirrel chattered in the tree above me. I looked up at the squirrel and then took out my Bowie knife and hammered with the butt of the knife on the trunk of the tree the squirrel was on. The squirrel leaped into space, and I was amazed, because it spread its arms and legs to create a surface much like a directional parachute. I watched it float through the air a very long way, down into a gully, where it disappeared into brush-like vegetation.

I was on my way to the Chinese Wall, as all the other backpackers called it. The Chinese Wall is approximately one thousand feet high and is a stone escarpment that goes relatively north and south for approximately twenty miles. I was able to see a grizzly bear in the distance, across a valley; it was reddish-brown in color. I knew that helicopters had been used to get the bear here after it got into trouble in a populated area. I just hoped that it would not bother me during the night.

Once, on a recent Sunday, when I was on the Auraria Campus near our home with my soccer ball (this one I have named Carmen), a robin flew straight at my head. I could have reached out and touched it. The robin was making a screeching noise that sounded almost like a call for help. Hot on its heels, intent on having lunch, was a falcon, which wisely veered away. Later, when I was done with my in-place exercises, I saw the robin and the falcon sitting side by side on the branch of a tree! As I ran by, trying to keep up with Carmen, I mused, "Now, isn't that the same set of birds?" I realized that this was an example of a natural, peaceful coexistence in which prey and predator are able to perch on the same branch of a tree. Then I decided that falcons would probably prefer to stun their prey in midair and the robin felt safe sitting on the same branch as the predator. I also came to the conclusion that when catching the robin in midair, the falcon would have both claws available to deal with its lunch, instead of risking its own life and limb by attacking the prey on the same branch. After all, on the branch it needed one leg to stand on!

Leaving Kings Canyon, in California, I stopped the car by a mountain river and prepared a sandwich that I ate with gusto. I allowed my eyes to wander, especially to the other bank. You would be surprised at the wildlife I have seen, employing this technique. I saw on the shore a little bird that I later learned was a water ouzel. He bobbed his tail about every three steps as he walked the length of the rock he was on, and then he proceeded right on into the water! The whole body, including head and shoulders, disappeared; then, a minute or so later, it reappeared upstream on the same rock! The bird happened to be on a shopping trip for a healthy water bug snack. With the incessant roar of the fast-moving creek, I would have thought the bird would be more wary of predators, but it wasn't. It bobbed its tail with every step it took. It was, feathers removed, about the size of a man's thumb, and it was the first I'd ever seen.

*   *   *

Throughout my adult lifetime, outdoor scenic photography has continually been a personal interest of mine, and this has added greatly to the pleasure of being outdoors.

In 1976, I used some of my photographs on homemade Christmas cards. One was *The Tiny Tannenbaum*, a photo of a young pine tree, about a foot high, in a forest of larger trees, all of which were balancing clumps of new snow and glistening in the sunlight. Another was *The Nearest Star*, a shot of several snow-covered spruce trees, with the sun looking like a star as captured by the camera lens. On the backs of the cards was a printed note saying, "Eye Opener Photos, by Jim Oliver."

I had various cameras over the years. I still have a large collection of photographs and 35mm slides from my hikes and travels, including from the year I was in Vietnam. Now I am trying to adjust to the digital age, the computer, and our own printer. I enjoy capturing the fantastic sunrises, sunsets and weather patterns (almost daily) that I can see from our home balconies.

This dedication to extensive photographing on a trail is one of the reasons I took up solo backpacking. Past partners would stamp their feet whenever I stopped because I saw something (be it flowers or scenery) that just needed to be photographed. They demonstrated impatience, even if nothing was said. It made me uncomfortable, and I didn't want to experience any more of their impatience. From that point on, I was always "too busy" and let them go by themselves—and I enjoyed the pleasure of going solo and taking photographs as I wished.

Solo Backpacking

When I was younger, I found solo backpacking to be much more appealing than going with a group (which consisted of one more than me). The reasons I preferred solo backpacking are several, although I must admit there were occasional times when I could have used someone's help.

I don't backpack anymore. I simply realized that I needed to give up one of the great pleasures of my life. (I gave away my backpack and small tent to the Disabled American Veterans about ten years ago.) I was just getting older and found that I could not cover the long distances I used to be able to cover energetically. There were other specific reasons I gave up backpacking: (1) when I bushwhacked across forests, I occasionally discovered someone's marijuana farm, and I could just feel the rifle on my temple, (2) I could no longer depend on youthful self-reliance to keep me out of trouble, and (3) the wilderness trails and campsite areas were starting to feel crowded.

My solo backpacking excursions in the 1970s and 1980s were mostly in remote areas where there were apt to be few people.

*   *   *

Bob Marshall Wilderness, Montana—1972: I encountered my first amazing flying squirrel and grizzly at night. Arriving back at the Gibson Reservoir, I turned on the *Pint*'s (my 1972 Ford Pinto) radio to hear that Israeli Olympians had been assassinated by terrorists—and right then, I immediately wanted to return to "the Bob!"

*   *   *

Sawtooth Wilderness, Idaho—Fall 1974: This whole area was an eye-opening challenge. I spent a great deal of my time taking photographs. One of them is on the wall of my and my wife's office today.

*   *   *

The High Uintas National Recreation Area, Utah—September 1977: It is a fact that this area in eastern Utah is huge! Its major mountain range is the only above-timberline mountain range in the United States that runs east–west.

I was caught in a snowstorm while backpacking the High Uintas—a few days past the Labor Day weekend, I believe. Snow was coming down fast, in very large, wet flakes. "This can't be," I protested to no one in particular. "This is spring snow! Then again, these are mountains!"

Soon I stopped fighting the rapidly accumulating snow, slogging through it, the backpack getting heavier by the minute with the wet and heavy flakes. I stopped and studied my topographic map. "Concentrate on what you're going to do next, Ollie Bear! It's decision time." Dead ahead of me about five miles would be the *Pint*, just where I had parked it three days before, my trusted steed that would take me to warmth and shelter—if I could really believe I could make it through this heavy stuff!

I remember visualizing some possible local newspaper headlines: "Body of Stupid Oliver Backpacker Found One Mile from Car." Then I thought of Mama and her stinging words to me as a kid back in the Philippines: "If you're going to die on me, then die like an Oliver. Get in the shade!" I remember her turning around and striding with purpose toward the farm home.

In spite of all these mental games, I knew that I was faced with what I term a survival-decision moment. After all, there were blue spruce trees all about, becoming increasingly indistinguishable by the moment because of the wet and heavy flakes. *The decision-making process sure takes a long time*, I remember thinking—even as I shucked my backpack off. I really knew what I had to do, long before I thought I had made up my mind.

It was then I knew I was slowly freezing to death, because I had stopped hiking and I had taken the time to study my topo (topographic map, that is), and had spent time pondering my situation regarding whether it would be worth an extra effort to continue slogging to my car through this impeding stuff or whether it would be worth going into survival-mode thinking.

I then remembered a general's admonition to me just before I boarded the civilian airplane that twelve hours later took me to my headquarters in Saigon and the Vietnam War: "Live to fight another day!" By this time, I was so tired that I just wanted to go to sleep, so I selected a snow-covered blue spruce next to where I had just dropped off my backpack and gingerly—so as not to disturb a heavy accumulation of snow—crawled under the canopy of its branches. I felt welcome next to its ten-inch trunk.

A blue spruce always welcomes visitors. A spruce is lonely, because its needles take a long, long time to decay and as spruce needles deteriorate, the resulting ground cover is so acidic that even insects find the environment uninhabitable. It was dry and I was finally out of the storm in my hideaway beneath the spruce branches.

The next day, I made it back to my parked car. I got the windows cleared and the engine started. I slowly pulled onto the road and, within a matter of a few minutes more, I found myself high-centering while driving the little 1972 Ford Pinto, which was not really designed for off-roading in winter conditions. This was a memorable backpack adventure, to say the least. Sometimes things just don't work out the way you plan.

* * *

Kings Canyon Wilderness, California—September 1978: Clearly there were nine pine trees—each about a foot in diameter—in the estimated two-foot-deep mountain stream, which was cold and rushing, the water clear. I was amazed! I asked myself, *How could pine trees, which are propagated by cones, grow as large as I am seeing and take root and remain sturdy and thrive without being washed away?* Two days later I told a ranger, who said he knew exactly the tree grove I was describing, and about the trees I had seen and photographed.

Then he related to me an incredible story that had to do with a local drought in prehistoric times that lasted for at least two hundred years—just long enough for pinecones to be watered by some seasonal moisture and grow into sturdy trees whose tap roots went very deep for residual moisture. And the little grove of pine trees survived. When the drought finally broke and water started rushing once more, the trees' roots had gone into the soil deeply enough to hold the trunks steadily against the onslaught of water.

My attitude changed. Here I had just comprehended a miracle in the making—while most people sat on a flat rock, a beer in hand, wondering about the price of carrots at the local grocery store. Whatever!

I sat in wonder, imagining the breaking of the prehistoric drought and water being plentiful once more. The ranger who explained all this had by now collected an audience of about fifty people, so he embellished his story a bit. I didn't mind as long as he stayed on track, which he did.

After a week of backpacking, I was leaving the world of nature and starting back to my home on the base when I learned that a major had been killed while flying a stealth fighter plane (Lockheed-Martin F-117 Stealth) out of Edwards AFB, in Nevada—located across the desert about fifty miles to the east of Kings Canyon. All the entrances and exits of the entire Kings Canyon Wilderness were closed to car and bus traffic for the next seven or so days, because parts and pieces of the airplane had been strewn all over the place. Those were the days when stealth technology was still highly classified, I always wondered if they ever found remains of the pilot, because the USAF personnel who searched for parts and pieces of the plane released no other details. My stay in the wilderness was extended unexpectedly for another week.

Finally, after we were released to leave the area, I made a roadside stop and learned some new information about the trees growing there. I was fascinated by the fact that pecan trees grew right next to peach trees. They evidently got their nutrition from the very same soil, which simply needed water to produce healthy crops. I bought some peaches—so juicy, the best I had ever tasted—from a fruit stand manned by a little Hispanic girl. Then I slobbered my way toward Vandenberg AFB California and my next military assignment.

* * *

Humbug Spires Wilderness, Montana—1980: This is a spectacular area with many prominent limestone columns (they're called batholiths) showing above the forest cover.

* * *

San Juan Mountains, Weminuche Wilderness Area, Colorado—Summer 1987: This backpacking trip included getting a ride into the wilderness on the Durango-Silverton narrow-gauge railroad and then dropping off at a special stop only for hikers and mountain climbers. We all headed in our separate directions and would pick up the train back to civilization several days later. For me, a literal highlight of this particular trip was to be able to reach the summit of one of Colorado's highest peaks, Mt. Eolus—elevation 14,085 feet.

*   *   *

Holy Cross Wilderness, Colorado—September 1989: This was the first night out on a trip that was going to include three more nights in the wilderness. I picked out a good camping spot and set up my tent. After my first night on the trail, the next morning I woke up to the complete silence that can only mean one thing—several inches of snow on the tent. Any sounds were soft and muffled. Especially odd was that the birds were silent.

I was confused at first, asking myself, "Do I go ahead, or do I go back now?" Remembering the experience I had in the High Uintas of Utah, I gathered up my tent and supplies and reluctantly headed back to the trailhead that I had just left the day before. After several hours of forcing my way along the snow-covered trail, I reached the forest service access road, which also was totally covered with deep snow. I had hiked only a short ways on the dirt road before I realized a pickup truck was heading toward me. The driver picked me up and explained he was simply doing a personal survey of the effects of an early snowfall. I was thinking, *Okay, great idea!* Bianca, his white dog, was a pet friend that accompanied him wherever he went with his pickup truck.

Bianca's owner left me with two Coors beers outside a ranger's cabin several miles down the road; it appeared to be locked for the season. I knew I had better get inside and get out of my shoes, which seemed frozen to my wooden-feeling feet. I went to the back of the cabin and found the latch open; there was no lock in sight. In the dark, I searched for another person but found no one.

I started massaging my frozen feet at 1900 (7:00 p.m.) and got my first sensations in them about 0100—an hour after midnight. That was close! The protection was greatly appreciated at this point. The cabin gave me a chance to warm up, and I had no problem sleeping on the bare concrete floor. It was disappointing, however, to cut my backpacking trip short.

Cold Turkey II

Limiting my drinking was something else. I just knew at the very beginning that I did not want to quit consuming alcohol, but I also knew that I would die soon if I continued at the rate I was drinking booze, beer, and wine. At the time, I was going through a case of beer, a liter of white wine, plus more than a liter of whiskey each week. That's seven days. If I did not have my whiskey and ice cubes at the end of each day, I would sweat and become agitated until fulfillment occurred, and then I would calm my nerves with a long drink of a mixture with enough alcohol in it to kill a young buffalo. It goes without saying or writing that I was an immediately available candidate for quitting alcohol and starting a rehabilitation program. Just in case there are a few people out there who want to quit drinking, what follows is an explanation of the program that worked for me.

1. The first thing I did was be introspective. Did I really want to quit? When would be a good start date? What was alcohol doing to my social life? What was my alcoholic behavior doing to my professional life? What I needed was to find the answers within myself to the all of these questions. Why did I want to limit my drinking?

2. Then I acted decisively. On the date I had established as a start date, I began my program. I did not tell anyone about it, because if I failed my own program, no one else would be the wiser; otherwise, I would have some difficult explaining to do.

3. I broke up the entire sole objective into easily achievable parts. Don't forget to pat yourself on the back for each step you achieve. This part is very, very important! Give yourself credit for achieving each little step in reaching your goal.

During introspection, management of my drinking emerged. The questions I asked myself were these: Can you manage to consume just one drink—all night long? Can you hold it close to yourself the entire evening without taking so much of a nip that you must have an immediate refill? The answer to both questions was of course a resounding yes. *Of course I can do what's expected!* I have not been specific about the subject of introspection with anyone, because it is a personal matter. There is no guidance that I can cite regarding introspection. Much more so than my quitting smoking and therefore improving my health, I suddenly had more money than I could shake a stick at! Far less booze meant more money in my pocket, so I simply invested the extra money I had suddenly acquired.

I have often thought that I may have missed the boat, because other people have spent so much money in the past on learning how to quit smoking and also how to quit drinking that maybe I also could have cashed in on book deals or some written instructions on how to quit smoking or how to limit drinking alcohol. Seriously, my process begins with breaking up the main objective into achievable steps. A person cannot simply say, "Today, I will quit smoking!" and then expect success. Much more likely, they have set themselves up for failure.

A Lasting Marriage

All my life, what I really wanted was a marriage that lasted longer than five years. In the past, each time I became involved in a serious relationship, I had sincerely hoped that it would lead to a lasting marriage. For some reason, I always felt that I could voice a personal opinion from within a strong marriage that I could not make from a less stable relationship.

A lasting marriage is what my wonderful wife Louise has given me. I had developed what I called a five-year fear, since neither of my previous marriages had lasted more than five years. Then I met my Louise in 1986. We dated for five years, and by the end of that period, nothing terrible had happened. So I set aside eighteen years of bachelorhood and the requisite period testing the five-year fear and was married once more in 1991. We continue to be very happy together, and I've frequently wondered where this fascinating woman was all my life. She simply explains that our relationship would not have worked out earlier in the times when we were focusing on our careers (she in Colorado ski area management, me in the US Air Force and ICBMs) and the demands of our young families. In April 2015 we celebrated our twenty-fourth anniversary as man and wife. Excellent!

I admire the administrative contributions of Louise, my wife and close partner, fellow world traveler, dining guest of honor, and computer-whiz who obviously understands the machines and what makes them tick much better than I do. She has been an excellent source of ideas as well as significant editor in development of this book. She has also been my daily reminder of tasks that have to be done, without being a nag about the business at hand. A dedicated and loving companion for a long time, she's also been my best friend for many more years than I had hoped for. (I have no doubt that two previous wives tried their best to live with me, because I must have been a difficult person to understand, yet Louise somehow managed to stay twenty-four years, and I hope she finds it in her heart to stay at least another twenty-four.) I couldn't have completed this project without her help. Besides being in love with her, I worship the very ground upon which she walks.

While walking along the sidewalks of Denver, Colorado, she and I have been stopped by total strangers who remark, "Couples should hold hands more often, like you two do." I'm not sure how we're supposed to hold each other's hands; nor am I certain what necessitated such comments from strangers. Once, a young woman aboard the Sixteenth Street Mall Shuttle asked us, "How long have you two been married?" At first I was surprised at her inquiry, and then I proudly told her, "Since spring of 1991." I was wondering what prompted her to ask such a question of strangers, when she simply responded, "I figured it wasn't very long ago." Then she looked out the window of the bus.

I was curious about the comment and didn't really understand, so I questioned Louise. She had this explanation for me: "The young woman probably is just having a bad day in her personal life, and everyone is looking for hope that a relationship can be lasting. I guess that is what we represent to others." Experiences such as this have been usually been positive for us as well as the inquiring people, so we've simply regarded them as nuances in our lives.

Our Travels

Vietnam (both North and South), Cambodia, Thailand, and Laos I've been in, and I have seen all I need to see of these countries. But traveling together with Louise, we have variously enjoyed many sites, people, and lands, including Hawaii, Canada, Mexico, the Fiji Islands, Austria, France,

Hungary, the Czech Republic, Italy, England, Romania, the Netherlands, Norway, Turkey, Denmark, Peru (including mysterious Machu Picchu and the enormous Amazon River), Costa Rica, India (and its beautiful Taj Mahal, whose immensity still amazes me), Brazil, Israel, the Suez and the Panama Canals (an entire book can be written on why the Panama Canal cannot have the same type of free-flowing feature as the Suez), Oman, Colombia, several Caribbean islands, Hong Kong, Panama (where China has invested heavily), Finland, China (where we hiked the Great Wall), and Egypt (where we explored the interior of the Great Pyramid of Giza). We've also chased down World's Fairs in Canada, Australia, Japan, Spain, Portugal, and Germany. In December 2000, we were in Argentina, and we then hiked major islands of Antarctica—our final continent of the seven in the world.

Instead of investing our money in a normal fashion, in which there is a monetary return, we have been fortunate to have the choice of investing in a different way. Louise and I wanted to see various parts of our big world and learn how people lived in different places. We have traveled extensively, and on a wall in our home is a map in which a red pin shows where we have been. The map is covered with lots of red pins!

What follows are some of the worldwide facts that I have found to be very intriguing and meaningful to me personally:

We learned that during the early development of Wellington, New Zealand, the mayor liked the names of London streets so much that he superimposed a street map of London upon his developing city in New Zealand. Thus, Hyde Park can be found in Wellington just as it is found in London. It is unfortunate that Wellington is mountainous, whereas London is flat.

On the back of Victoria Peak outside of Hong Kong, China, there is a large hillside hotel. Designed into the middle of the complex is a huge hole, because the dragon has to have access to the sea. In other words, the dragon that lives on the mountain range all the time, will need a way, one fine day, to get to the sea unimpeded. This is a costly feature of the hotel, but woe betide the man who blocks the dragon from easily getting to the sea.

In Portugal there is a yellow line that is painted around many homes. This line prevents evil spirits from going from the ground into the house.

In Istanbul, Turkey, there is a widespread belief in the evil eye, so everyone we talked to carried an amulet to ward off the evil eye.

In Easter Island, the statues, which may look the same to you, the reader, do not all face out to the sea in anticipation of an expected arrival of who knows what. Instead, all statues face toward the village, in honor of the chief and villagers that sponsored each of them.

In Cologne, Germany, the Cathedral of Cologne was the only building left standing after Allied bombing raids of World War II. Obviously, the hand of God protects its own. In the real world, the commander of each bombing raid told the radar bombardier that the Cathedral of Cologne was the only building left standing from which bombardiers could sight their Norden bombsights during subsequent bombing raids.

In Antarctica during World War II, special operation Tabarin was initiated at Deception Island. This required a British major to head up a team of thirty personnel to prevent German U-boats from using stored leftover whale oil for fuel. An earlier British team had discovered that a U-boat had already used some stored whale oil.

In the province of Galicia, located in the upper right shoulder of Spain, bagpipes are a part of the culture. Many of the population wear kilts like Scottish people do. They play English games, such as Cricket, for instance. The one big difference is that they all speak Spanish.

In New Zealand, we saw a blooming Christmas tree, or pohutukawa. It is a bush-like flowering tree that grows quite large. The flower looks like a bottlebrush flower, but it is white in the center. The tree blooms only around Christmastime in December.

The Iditarod Trail Sled Dog Race covers 1,300 miles and is run every year beginning on the first Saturday of the month of March, from Anchorage to Nome, Alaska. In March of 1996, Louise and I participated in the mushers' dinner at the community recreation center, which is held several days prior to the race. It was after dinner that we saw a lead dog of some past winner urinate on the trophy after sniffing it carefully. Such an irreverent act by the dog amused the audience greatly, and was described by the master of ceremonies as "kicking the trophy."

In Antarctica, we saw a colony of penguins on one of the islands. We turned to a staff member with us and asked, "How many penguins in that colony?"

He matter-of-factly looked and said, "Oh, a quarter of a million." We were amazed at his answer and at the abundance of wildlife in Antarctica.

At Easter Island, Chile is the administrative country. If you look at maps showing time zones, New York City is in the same time zone as Santiago, Chile. Therefore, Easter Island (several thousand miles to the west) is on the same time zone as Santiago, Chile.

In 1990, Louise and I visited Japan, generally the Kyoto area. I asked our tour guide, a Japanese citizen, about Kokura, which had been a primary target for the second atom bomb in World War II. She politely responded, "Those who lived in Kokura at that time developed a guilty conscience about the war. They felt like they had not taken their knocks like the rest of Japan had, especially those who lived in Hiroshima." When Kokura was cloud-covered, the bombers were diverted to the secondary target instead, and that was Nagasaki.

At Hiroshima we learned that just thirty days after their World War II atomic bombing, new oleander bushes were already seen poking up through soil and cracks in the sidewalks at ground zero. This was the area that nuclear experts had said would see no new life for many years to come. Evidently, a typhoon that hit the area shortly after the bombing had washed great amounts of the radioactive materials out to sea.

In Zambia during 2012, we learned that parents can be very stoic about the loss of their ten-year-old daughter to a river crocodile. The only available water for the village came from the river, and they simply did their best to avoid the crocodiles.

The southern coast of Portugal is the Algarve, where millionaires from Europe go seasonally. All over the country, we saw almond trees. In the spring, the falling petals cover the ground like snow, and there is a common legend about a princess who likened them to snow.

War Story Number Seven

Just before going to Iraq in 2007, my son CW4 James, usually an instructor pilot for the Kansas National Guard but doing some flying for the US Army, was sent TDY to a flying training program over the California plains just west of Yosemite National Park. In a C-23 Sherpa aircraft, he was trained to fly fairly long distances at an altitude of fifty feet or lower. This procedure was born of a tactical need generated by the Iraq War.

Previously, C-23s used to take off from air bases in Iraq under their normal-use technical data, which called for a five-thousand-foot altitude gain just passing the end of the runway. These procedures were good until a copilot was chain-gunned with .30-caliber bullets on the underside of his right leg by Iraqi insurgents at the end of the runway. He survived, but procedures changed. Now, in any takeoff by a US Army C-23 Sherpa in Bagram AB, the pilot lines up his aircraft in the landing end of the runway, guns down the runway using full military power all the way, takes off, and then, since the plane has short takeoff and landing (STL) capability, lifts off long before the end of the runway and banks left or right. The pilot flies at an altitude of fifty feet for five miles, and then (and only then) climbs to his normally prescribed altitude of five thousand feet. Procedures are normal after that.

The OBCR (Ollie Bear Cousins Reunion)

In late December of 2011, my brother Bob, now the patriarch of the family, updated several generations of us by discussing the little red hen cookie jar that had been part of Grandma's household icons at the Corners Farm. He also had with him Trilby's horse-skin "blanket" that we slept under on cold nights during Indiana winters. Because of these and various other items, a simple family gathering became a wondrous learning situation for several generations of cousins, and a cookie jar and a horse blanket assumed center stage for the curious among us.

Trilby, we learned, was the name of the Oliver family horse when Papa was yet a child; he grew up with the horse. When Trilby died of old age, Grandma Hively (Papa's mother) missed her devoted pet so much that she directed a local taxidermist to tan Trilby's hide and convert it into a blanket, which has now become a fascinating family heirloom.

In Grandma's Hively's living room was a little red hen cookie jar; it frequently was almost empty. Grandma died when she was about eighty-five years old, and no one knew what happened to the cookie jar. It had simply disappeared. Then, several years later, Bob learned of an estate sale to be held when one of our aunts died in Muncie, Indiana. He was curious, it was a bright Sunday afternoon, and he likes to drive, so he attended the auction. One of the items he discovered to be auctioned was the little red hen cookie jar! He concluded that Aunt Densie had simply taken it with her after visiting grandma (her mom, of course), and value being in the eye of the beholder only, she knew that passing it on to her own children would be meaningless, because at the time they were deeply involved in very important matters in their lives. So my brother Bob bought the cookie jar for five dollars, and it became his to keep forever.

And what about the "Ollie Bear" title of our family gathering? When an English-derived word such as our surname, Oliver, is pronounced by a Spanish speaker, it becomes "Ollie Burr." That's because the *v* consonant in English sounds like a *b* when it's pronounced by a Spanish speaker. So it wasn't a giant leap of imagination to come up with Ollie Bear. The family gathering was therefore called the Ollie Bear Reunion.

Spanish as a language is widespread in the Philippines; the fact has been incontrovertible since 1520, when Spanish explorer Ferdinand Magellan made a stopover at Mactan Island in the Visayan region during his circumnavigation of the world. Magellan also died there. The year 1520 is also when the Philippines was Christianized (concerned citizens of Akron, Indiana, notwithstanding). History tells us that Magellan was killed on Mactan Island during a skirmish precipitated by politicians involving a local chief, king, or datu named Lapu-Lapu. (We have lost track of relatives in the Philippines who could corroborate a family assertion that, since her birthplace was so close to Magellan's landing site, our mama is related to King Lapu-Lapu.)

First Aid for PTSD—SST

PTSD is the abbreviation of post-traumatic stress disorder. Several times when I compiled or wrote of events described in this book, I experienced emotional effects I could not explain. These were events that I had put out of my mind since childhood, and now to write about them for this book forced me to deal with them as an adult. This is one of the reasons that developing the content of this book has taken several years. I was introduced to these feelings during some of the final conversations I had with my sister, Becky. I realized then that some of our childhood horrors had continued to haunt her throughout her life (and she didn't even know the reason). For example, she explained to me that whenever she would hear a siren, she could not prevent tears rolling down her face.

Seeing current interest in and headlines about PTSD, I began to understand and accept how this had affected my own life. After earlier wars, these symptoms were called shell shock, and combat fatigue. PTSD has probably been around since humans have walked the earth. Only in recent times has the term PTSD been used and specific efforts made to overcome the issues of the affliction, both mental and physical.

In my case, I am probably suffering from PTSD that originated not only from wartime as an adult (specifically, Vietnam), but also from my childhood experiences growing up during WWII in the Philippines. While trying to understand and overcome my personal symptoms and reactions that contribute to the condition, I have also learned more about PTSD in general. For instance, my observations include the fact that a child tends to simply go on with life with no alternative but to totally ignore what has happened in the past; no one else is likely to even take notice. An adult, on the other hand, tends to consciously push the memories into the background and conjure up excuses that never meet the stressor head-on. This is the reason that if you are given a choice of trying to understand the background of an adult or a child, it is easier to do so with the adult, because at least you will get an idea that there is some sort of a problem and have a chance of determining what is behind all the excuses. For example, we've all heard of grandkids asking, "What did you do during the war?" and Grandpa avoiding answering the inquiry by insisting that he has to go to the golf course or the American Legion Hall, or somewhere else, right now. Another example: One day Louise and I were at the local Christkindl Market, and a young vendor, noticing my USAF cap, shared with us that she wished she had had an opportunity to talk to her grandpa about a box of his medals that she found in the basement. He had always made some sort of a legitimate excuse to avoid the subject. He just couldn't talk about his medals and wartime experiences.

While writing this memoir, I have been able to develop a personal first aid approach for countering the effects of PTSD that has been helpful for me. I call it SST, and that stands for "sort, select, talk." I will briefly share the process that has been helpful for me.

1. **Sort:** This first step is to begin breaking down the experience or time period into pieces that can be sorted. That is where trying to outline and plan for this book came into play. I hadn't really thought of the individual terrifying aspects; any mental reference at all was rather broad. A chronological listing of what went on during those times will eventually bring out some of the most hidden of memories. The list was short at first (just the title of the book), and then, slowly, the list got longer and more complete.

2. **Select:** Once the PTSD experience was broken into identifiable pieces, I could look at each one as a manageable entity to think about and eventually gain understanding of. No longer was it just a ghost of the past.

3. **Talk:** The final step is to talk about each detail. Again, in my case, I found that writing about it was excellent as well. The more difficult and damaging the aspect seems, the longer you may need to talk and write about it. It helps to have a partner to listen and just let you talk, or to review your writing.

Somehow, through this step-by-step first aid approach, the very confusing and emotionally demanding issues that I've been dragging along with me seem to settle down enough to permit going about day-to-day life with more energy and a little more lighthearted. I would have to say it is never too late to benefit from SST.

*   *   *

Warren Jackson and his wife, Donna, are my dear brother and sister-in-law. They have both been personally influential, especially in my later years. People with the individual trait of kindness are indeed rare. Countless times, Louise and I have been invited to their home to participate in political discussions and to share Donna's delicious cooking. Warren is always very generous with his time and endless energy. We enjoy the sharing of his numerous and various adventures—from projects with the Boy Scouts to impressive catering manager responsibilities. Warren's college degree is from the University of Colorado, in political science. For many years he was a Boy Scout leader supreme. Two years ago we attended ceremonies at his retirement from scouting. But other would-be

Boy Scout leaders still seek Warren out for his organizing ability. In this regard, Warren has gotten himself into an enviable situation in which he has retired and yet cannot retire. A recent record-breaking achievement of his in the state of Colorado is the organizing of a board of review for the twelfth Eagle Scout Award candidate he has worked with and steered toward the award in 2012. I have had the opportunity to meet a few of these young men and have been impressed that they are so mature for such young ages. Each time I meet one, I have a reassurance that as we elders go our separate ways because of old age, the world will be left in good hands.

Donna is a retired teacher, having taught and graduated many elementary school students—including several who returned years later to visit her, their favorite teacher. Among this massive horde of appreciative returnees was a young military officer of the US Naval Academy at Annapolis, Maryland. She attended the University of Northern Colorado and then Regis University here in Denver, Colorado, where she earned a master's degree in education.

* * *

Eric and Heidi are Louise's grown-up children. Eric now directs the Reliability Engineering branch of a huge international corporation supporting the US automotive industry. Heidi works full-time for a security surveillance company while keeping up with her family, which consists of her husband, Patric, and two kids. Cheyenne is a university student in California, working on a degree in graphic design and Logan is an exceptional ice hockey goalie and an honor-roll high school student. In the current high-technology field of computers, both Cheyenne and Logan are super savvy when it comes to their use. I marvel at how far our civilization has progressed simply through use of computers, with the younger generation leading the way.

* * *

Attorney Edward C. Fensholt and his wife, Renee, from Kansas, are welcome to my part of Colorado anytime. One evening in July 2012, we stopped near our home to help a couple of obvious visitors to town locate their destination on a map they were studying with confused looks. We visited briefly, and then they invited us to join them for dinner in the restaurant across from us. Enjoying much conversation after dinner, we closed down the restaurant. Both Ed and Renee are superb ambassadors who represented their home state of Kansas well. They are unquestionably proponents of the Golden Rule. Bless both of them for being such nice people. Louise and I easily came to the conclusion that Ed and Renee are living examples of grace and tolerance.

*　*　*

Wayne Coulton Frieling and Kylie Sue Frieling are fraternal twins, the children of wonderful people—Mitzi and Wayne in Manhattan, Kansas. The twins both had a rough go of it when they were born; both needed respirator assistance for several weeks. We met Mitzi on one of our early international travels and have kept in touch ever since. Christmas newsletters keep us up to date on the latest news and about the family accomplishments.

*　*　*

Cindy Scott-Johnson, very recently remarried to computer whiz David, is a young mom who has been providing us home care and cleaning every month for the past twenty years. In that time, she went to college and in nine years earned a bachelor of science degree in anthropology, was married, and bore two children: Cassie Tanner and Jeremiah Tanner. Cindy has also earned certification as a provider of home care of her severely handicapped child, while at the same time she holds down daily employment responsibilities. As a single parent, she skillfully managed the ongoing challenges of her little family. My wife and I were pleased to be invited to her recent wedding when she married a wonderful partner who cares for her kids as if they were his own.

Concluding Thoughts

All that a happy man who's writing his memoir needs around him is a happy wife!

Food Is Food

During the start of the war, we were always hungry, and food was not available in any form or way. That is probably why none of us Oliver siblings understand why people laugh when Hollywood movies depict a so-called food fight. It is not funny. I cannot laugh when Hollywood includes food-fighting scenes in a movie. In fact, I find the situation rather insulting—a back-handed slap to the face of God.

I will always remember the word *"Bwisit."* It is Visayan for one who plays with his food, and it has special meaning for me. "Bwisit" is a pejorative word. It is also used for one who calls his food indelicate terms.

Today I would be the worst gourmet food critic in the world, because to me, *all* food is good. There were so many times between December 1941 and September 1945 that I just stayed around the house simply because I was hungry and I thought maybe Mama would magically come up with something to give to us kids. I am half proud and half guilt-stricken about some of my thoughts and expectations as a child, regarding regular availability of something (anything!) to eat. Now my attitude is that *food is food!*

Nicknames Abound

I have a natural inclination to give names to objects around me, including plants, soccer balls, and other things, such as family cars. Once a thing receives a name, there's some degree of personalization that's brought into play. To give a name to an inanimate object is to ascribe a soul to it.

In this way, I am like the Inuit Eskimos. They are fanatical about assigning names to stars and even grains of sand (which in number do not even come close to the number of stars in the sky). Nevertheless, I have named our plants, soccer balls, and other things—because it seems to me that names are much more useful and certainly more personal than otherwise.

All houseplants have personalities, and in my home, they have names too. Over a period of several months, I enjoyed a daily celebration with our potted plants. Each morning, with a great deal of show and fanfare, one deserving plant was chosen and openly announced as the plant of the day, or the plant du jour, or some reference would be made regarding the PDJ Award. Quite an honor, I'm sure.

Alphonse was named that only because he looks like an Alphonse; otherwise he's a dracaena, or just a common corn plant. Unfortunately, he grew tall and ungainly. I cut the tall stalk of Alphonse the plant, according to the nursery recommended plan, and watered the separate pots as the separate plants grew. The most successful was the original Alphonse, who retained three stalks, each replete with its root networks deeply embedded in its own soil—without its experiencing trauma except for the lack of original leaves.

Rattles—well, it's a snake plant! What else could we name it? Its leaves are many, with some as tall as we are, and that is over five feet, six inches!

How about our handy wire cart on wheels that we use for hauling groceries, laundry, or whatever, up and down our building elevator? It is black and has the name of Boston—or Bostie, for short—named after a vintage detective movie character named Boston Blackie.

More common, perhaps, are owners who name their favorite cars. Old Reliable comes to mind, and also Tenderfoot. The Blaze (1972 Chevy Blazer), Big Blue (1970 Oldsmobile Toronado), and the Pint (1972 Ford Pinto) happen to be the names Louise and I gave our early 1970s vintage vehicles when she and I first met in 1986. Previously I owned a Gray Ghost (1962 Chevy).

In the last year, I've also given names to the support canes that help me get around. At first there was Louise's fine trekking pole, which has been accompanying her for many years and was named Bonnie when I began using a matching pole I called Clyde. Then came Jock, a collapsible cane that sort of stands up on a swiveling base (and used to have a handy two-way flashlight to show the way at night, until the unreplaceable batteries wore out). Then I found a new sturdy, stand-up friend in Buddy, the stately quad-cane, and next was Suzie-Q (another quad-cane when I needed even more stability). My two walking sticks that look like ski poles and go outside with me are named Remus and Romulus. This is my team of assistants that keep me upright and moving ahead—each with a name, of course!

Bully for You

In the United States, I have frequently met fellow citizens who share with me a great deal of mutual respect. Most of these citizens have a sense of nation in which each member contributes to the well-being of the rest. There are a few exceptions, however—individuals who do not add to the wealth of the nation. Instead, by their speech and behavior, they create unkind and unnecessary issues that should receive the respectful attention of everyone. These are the bullies and racists, as our culture is currently naming them.

I have reserved this particular section of my memoir to point out that racist bullying continues in many aspects of life in this country, in spite of what is written on the Statue of Liberty. We think that bullying only goes on in the classrooms of the young, but I can tell you it is spread from corner to corner of our country and continues from the cradle to the grave.

In my view, racists are cowards because they remain hidden from public scrutiny yet take swipes at their targets without displaying their hatred of the differences between themselves and the objects of their bullying.

The top reasons for this superiority that specific people assume—and that I have observed—are differences in race, religion, gender, physical condition, and mental condition. Just because we are humans, we naturally suspect someone because he or she possesses features that are different from those that we personally possess. Fortunately, individuals generally outgrow those suspicions as we become mature.

After researching the subject, I would define racial prejudice as an illogical and irrational hatred of those who possess features different from those owned by the hater. In other words, just because you are different in one fashion or another, the deck is stacked against you. This description sounds very much like attempts by a bully to demean an individual whom he wishes to dominate and eventually make his victim.

In chapter 3, I wrote about the insulting sermon I witnessed. In those Akron, Indiana, schoolboy years, I wouldn't have known what the reverend was really stating in his Sunday talk. Back then I was just a brown-skinned kid. Today, at the age of seventy-eight, I am a retired lieutenant colonel in the US Air Force, a retired ICBM squadron commander, holder of a master's degree in public administration, an author of two books, and a loyal taxpayer who simply acknowledges God and is a man of God. None of these qualifications came to me freely, none arrived early or late, and none came to me just because I held out an open hand. I had to work and earn each one! That's why I don't forget to mention them often to other people, and lest I be taken to be cheap, I don't trade them for a moment of glory either.

It is an unfortunate circumstance that my mama, who had skin of a different color because she was from the Philippines, decided to walk out on the reverend's sermon. She had not known that she was in the United States of America, one of the most racially prejudiced countries in the world. I say this from the experience of seeing one US federal government form after another ask me what race I was! After a great deal of conjecture, I generally check the box labeled "other"—and why not? After all, the US Air Force did not ask me what race I was when it appointed me commander of the 90 OMMS.

I experienced a typical racist bullying incident a few years after retiring from the air force when I walked into the neighborhood office of the Division of Motor Vehicles to renew my driver's license. They were doing some presorting of the usual confused crowd coming through the doors, and the government employee pointed at me and called out, "Do you have your green card?" I noticed they did not ask the same question of my wife, Louise, who has blue eyes and fair skin.

"Overly sensitive," some would say. My response would be that racist bullying is never appropriate or justified in any way, shape, or form—or at any age. I can tell you that it never ends and is a societal disease that needs to be eradicated.

*   *   *

My Papa's advice after a university professor made offensive racist remarks in one of my classes and I complained to him was this: "The best way to fight public discrimination is to go silently about improving yourself. Get a good education, achieve goals, get certified for your skills, and collect trophies for your exceptional performance. Then your accomplishments will be plainly evident and people will be too embarrassed to openly discriminate against you. More than that, you will have proved to yourself that what they are saying is wrong, and you can just continue to be proud of the fine person you have become."

*   *   *

"Who says we're normal?" My brother Bob responded several years ago when I philosophically stated, "You know, considering all that has happened to us, it's a wonder we turned out normal." He fixed me with an accusatory eye and was ready for an argumentative discussion. I have continued to think about my brother's reaction to my comment, and I conclude he indeed has a point worth pondering.

There commonly exists among all of us a notion that normalcy is akin to beauty being in the eye of the beholder, that the answer is within those of us who survive our own little wars—not only a big one, such as the one we siblings had experienced firsthand. What is inherent in my brother's response is that normality is a condition perceived by our culture to be a standard—especially of behavior. Those few in our culture who exhibit behavior that is contrary to a standard that has been established are not normal; they are abnormal. So we are normal if, outwardly at least, we demonstrate characteristics to meet the standard set by society. If our demonstrations don't match that standard, then our society will inevitably brush us away. Since we usually don't want to be gotten rid of, we adhere to the standard.

I have concluded that we Oliver kids (a widely used general reference, inasmuch as we have grown much older) are normal, to the extent that we outwardly exhibit characteristics of normalcy that meet the standard established by our society. After many years of personal observation, I can assure you that individuals of our family group have expended much effort and done our best to be normal in our culture. If we are perceived to be otherwise, that's a problem of the beholder. In other words, it's your problem, not mine.

Personal Convictions

My wife, Louise, and I live in a condominium on the thirty-ninth floor of Brooks Tower, which is a forty-two-floor residential skyscraper in downtown Denver, Colorado. I often ponder the strokes of luck that brought me, at my age of seventy-eight years and in this stage of life, to this wonderful home in downtown Denver. Here I am, after experiencing and participating in three wars and living in jungle nipa huts in my early childhood. Introspectively, I usually wind up telling myself out loud, "Ollie Bear, it all has to do with some people being lucky and some being unlucky. You happen to be one of the lucky ones; that's all."

But no, it's much more than that. It has much to do with being honest with oneself, being resourceful, and applying those convictions and traits at the right time. Over the years, a few individuals might have believed I was born with a so-called silver spoon in my mouth. Well, that's certainly not a correct perspective. The presumption is far from the truth. In fact, life has not been easy for me; I have experienced rough times as well, especially when I was simply growing up!

There are two very wise sayings that express my attitude toward life: "Always be true to yourself" and "Everything happens in its own time." The first is about honesty and reminds me that I must always honor my own beliefs. The next tones things down a little bit to remind me that I don't have control over everything in my life and that I must respect a greater power and also my own physical limitations.

*   *   *

In downtown Denver, Colorado, approximately five years ago, around dusk on a hot Friday evening in spring, Louise and I were heading home after running a few errands in a Denver mall. Coming around the corner at the intersection of Champa and Sixteenth Streets, I almost stepped on a small foil balloon; it was somewhat flat in design and about eight inches in diameter, but it was inflated. Then the realization hit me that we had just passed a frantic woman loaded down with a briefcase, a couple of wrapped gifts, and the balloon we had just discovered. We surmised the harried mom was on her way home to celebrate a long-awaited birthday evening with her young child.

We looked down the block ahead of us just as an end-of-the-day Regional Transportation District (RTD) bus was coming to its designated stop to pick up its share of the thousands of people who work in downtown Denver each day of the workweek. From a distance, we helplessly watched as the mom boarded the bus unaware that she had lost the balloon she was hoping to add to birthday festivities—perhaps the first—for her child. It made us sad to think that her plans would not quite work out. I took home the discovery, and after several years it still resides in a corner of our dining room, a reminder of the dedicated love of a mother for her child.

The birthday balloon speaks to us about the day it was lost, but its mission to spread good feelings and good cheer is not gone. Many years ago, when we discovered the lost balloon, Louise and I made a promise that it would continue to be in the midst of a celebration—a celebration without end—sitting with our library shelf of books yet to be written. After several years, the birthday balloon still resides on the shelf, this time with other books that are stored in a corner of our dining room. Whenever I see the combination, I am reminded of the dedication of a busy mother to her child. I am at peace with the universe whenever I see our birthday balloon, still inflated, for it could easily have been lost forever had Louise and I not been there at that single moment, as breezes in a city blow in various directions and at various strengths, which we have noticed over the years we have lived downtown. The birthday balloon continues to celebrate birthdays even today.

*   *   *

I have been self-taught concerning the world of personal financial investments. At first I started by reading financial magazines, talking to buddies at the officers' club—getting the terms and general ideas pinned down. I soon migrated toward a concentration on understanding and comparing no-load equity mutual funds. Early on, I got the idea of staying in a fund for the long term, and I avoided jumping around to change an investment unless I had a really good reason to do so. When Louise and I became an investing team in the 1980s, we were both earning good salaries and were able to make regular, substantial monthly contributions to our choice of funds, which grew nicely over the years. Our financial goals and day-to-day requisite expenses were similar. For example, we were each perfectly happy to be driving our 1972 vehicles in 1986, not concerned about the miles that had accumulated. They just kept rolling along and indirectly contributed to our management of family finances.

Rather than preaching about the details, over the years, Louise and I hoped we could just be an example of how a couple of hardworking, rather frugal (every now and then) individuals could be ready to handle the challenging fiscal environment of retirement. We feel fortunate to be living in the location and community of our choice, and specifically residing in a nice condominium with conveniences and services that we greatly appreciate as we get older.

It has been wonderful to have the physical and financial ability to enjoy our regular domestic and international travels. Louise has had a chance to utilize her organizing and creative inclinations at home to create thirty-three magnificent Chronicle scrapbooks that cover in detail each trip we have taken. Most reference books cover typical two-week-duration trips, but quite a number cover in detail the fifty-two-day, fifty-one-day, and thirty-five-day trips we have taken. Now, when we are not taking the long trips anymore, reviewing the scrapbooks is a pleasurable experience in itself.

*   *   *

In its own fashion, the international political forces that caused the Kamala Circus (which I attended in the Philippines) to fold in the mid-1950s are one and the same as those found in US politics today. Its objectives are the same thread—and those are to get as many favorable nods as possible for the effort expended. In US politics today, an excellent trade-off is the kudos given to the politician who receives a pound of favorable nod, especially from the constituency, in return for expending an ounce of effort. So it is the American voter who gives final approval to a politician's or political candidate's efforts. It is not the politician's fault if matters turn out badly; it is the voter's fault for putting the politician in a position where his behavior and activities are not quite up to the standards we would expect.

*   *   *

My medical philosophy is that one should give the body a chance to heal itself; that's how one gets well from any sickness. It's not what the doctor does to you that makes you well; it's a great deal more likely that the medical practitioner does something that buys time and encourages conditions in which the body is able to heal itself. The doctor decreases your discomfort while your body heals itself.

*   *   *

I call my concept of aging Ollie-bear-itis, and it falls in line with what I have read about the natural process of dying, which probably starts the day we are born. I have learned that there are subsystems in the human body, and getting to an old age just wears them out. So, despite the fact that I am seventy-eight years old, I have often fallen, and I have had prostate cancer, surgery, and many other malfunctions of the body. The doctor and hospital staff continue to ply me with diagnoses and medicines as if I am sick with some mysterious disease that they, at least, know! I have had MRIs of the brain (the doctor hopes to catch a tumor growing in my head). I have been sent to specialists who teach me how to swallow and teach me what exercises I need to keep from falling.

I contend that I'm just getting old and my systems are worn out. Maybe that is why I don't have as much energy as I used to have! It is unfortunate that there is not a named disease for *getting old*. This is the reason I call my condition Ollie-bear-itis, while the medical staff, I believe, are treating me for a suspected specific disease they are compelled to define.

*   *   *

I need to express my gratitude to some fine medical practitioners who have helped me both physically and mentally. They and their medical staffs have helped me to remain happy and healthy into my old age (and my wife, too!) At the University of Colorado Health Center, John C. Scott, MD (retired), was our first primary health care provider at the UCH Senior's Clinic, followed by Maria Vejar, MSM, GNP; Albaha Barqawi, MD, UCH / Urology (Oncology), dealt with my prostate cancer; Christine Finlayson, MD, UCH, was Louise's breast cancer surgeon; Peter Kabos, MD, UCH / Breast Center (Oncology), Louise's follow-up oncologist; Lauren Seebergeer, MD, UCH, a specialist in neurosciences and movement disorders. Others outside of UCH include our dentist and good friend for so many years James R. Gatz, DDS; Kenneth Ridder, OD, who checks our vision every year; and Dr. Nancy Shubat, clinical psychologist and friend, for helping me adjust when I returned from the Vietnam War. I acknowledge all these people for their professionalism and their high measure of motivation. As health providers, they are all highly skilled and wonderful individuals as well.

A Final Tribute

With the death of little sis, we remaining three (my brothers Bob and Winston, and I) now compose half the number of WWII Oliver miraculous survivors. I continue to be ever so grateful to my parents for their efforts to make certain we four kids survived WWII and adjusted to our social environment after the war. I am grateful to them for giving me a chance to live as I wished, including the ability and opportunity to write a collection of memories. I have often pondered how I could have become a tranquil seventy-eight years old and achieved such a peaceful life without their help and loving concern. I conclude I couldn't have.

On weekends, whenever I am near a church, no matter the denomination, I go inside. At those times, I sit with my soccer ball (running companion) and whimsically wonder how I was so lucky to become as old as I am and why I do what I am doing. Frequently I am the sole occupant in the church. I sit in silence and contemplate the solemnity of its interior and study its architectural work and design. Then, in the quiet darkness and serenity that surrounds me, I silently talk with my parents. I thank them—but mostly I thank my mama, because she was the only one during the big war who could make things happen—for their efforts to give me a chance. I know they both sacrificed much, and I want them to know I am grateful. I thanked them while they were alive, but I didn't thank them enough. I realize more than ever that everything I have experienced in my lifetime could not have happened without a great deal of love and self-sacrifice on their part. After I have expressed a prayerful appreciation to my parents, I conclude with the promise that we will meet in spirit again soon—perhaps from some other quiet place. I leave the church with a lighter heart.

In his later years, Papa was laid low by stroke. After so many years of living one adventure after another, he was confined to a wheelchair for five years. I have found it ironic that he had walked the earth as an adventurer—a tiger with boundless energy and freedom to roam—only to be confined to a wheelchair during his last years. After his stroke in 1961, Mama cared for him daily until his death of a heart attack on a chilly, overcast morning—Sunday, March 20, 1966.

After Papa was gone, Mama lived twenty additional years in our lonely Corners Farm home, until she too died—many say of old age, but I say of a broken heart. You will comprehend my meaning after you have read my explanation, which follows.

I'm convinced Mama was very lonely during her last years. Most of the time, the only nearby friends she had were her pet cats and an occasional mouse that came in from the fields. When her pets died of some malady, the ground in Indiana was often difficult to dig into—especially in winter, when it was either snow-covered or frozen so hard that it was impossible to dig a hole in the ground large enough for a pet's carcass. So especially during an Indiana winter, where does one temporarily keep the body of a dead pet? Especially if one has become too old to dig a hole in frozen ground? In an emptied vegetable compartment of the refrigerator, of course!

Between assignments in my military career, I would come by for a once-in-a-while hello. Oh, I so much regret now that I didn't find the time to see my mama more often at our little home at the Corners Farm! During one of my visits, I opened the refrigerator and discovered inside an emptied compartment containing the carcass of a pet cat. Its carcass was already ceremoniously wrapped in waxed paper, and I have no doubt that the very process of preparing the body for eventual disposal had been heartrending. At the moment, I imagined that many a tear had already been shed in lonely darkness over the premature departure of the beloved pet.

At the time of my surprising discovery, I chose to mask my consternation over the whole issue, because I was not privy to the underlying reasons behind it. I didn't throw a temper tantrum or even ask questions that I could later classify as stupid, but I do remember my perplexity and initial dismay. Then I found myself feeling glad about the whole situation. I guess I was glad through empathy. Things just had to be the way they were, just as I had found them.

I was probably glad because of a selfishness of sorts; I didn't have to face the same situation or make the decisions my mama did. I now also believe I was glad, because at the time, I was afraid I might have come up with the same solution and moved in the same direction she did. But it had been her problem, not mine. That's how fundamental the situation really was. After all, I also remember that snow banks can melt overnight in Indiana, while several weeks later, the ground can still be frozen rock-hard. And what if she simply disposed of a dead pet by digging a hole in a soft snow bank and then the snow melted away during the night only to expose the carcass once more? Under those circumstances, I imagined she would still face disposal of a dear pet's carcass, but now it would perhaps be wet and dirty too. After the morbid discovery, I simply concluded that she had done what had to be done.

*   *   *

Papa and Mama lived a simple life at the Corners Farm; I think they did so because they were so financially poor. Yet once in a while during my college years, I would receive in the mail a small bread-and-butter note from them asking how I was doing, how school was, and whether activities were keeping me busy. Among the folds of the note, I occasionally found a five-dollar bill or a ten, and once in a while maybe even a one. (I used to call them an "Abe" [for Abraham Lincoln, whose face adorns a five-dollar bill], a "Ham" [for Alexander Hamilton on the ten], or a "George" [for George Washington on the one].) Among so many values I was learning to appreciate, those letters turned out to be such nice little surprises.

I only wish I had been more generous to my parents when I began earning my own money. My first job after graduating from Purdue University was cleaning out the men's toilet room at a very large steel mill complex located north of Gary, Indiana. Six months later, I started my air force career as a second lieutenant, and nobody would be awestruck by the military salary scale. Even though at the time, I already had a wife and small child, any amount of money I sent to my parents would have been of help to them. I would not have cared how they spent it; I just should have sent more, and I regret that I didn't!

My parents expected each of their children to finish high school and then continue on to college. Their influences were so indelibly ingrained in our minds that even as we reached adulthood, we didn't question why we were enrolled in academic institutions. It had been simply spelled out by both of them that they had expected each of us to continue our educational endeavors. So, like automatons, we simply enrolled in school and then went to work on our courses. Of course, my parents' expectations were high, perhaps whetted by a war merely a few years past that all of us had barely survived. But that is also why the three oldest kids eventually graduated from college with hard-earned degrees in our clenched fists. Those pieces of paper—I later referred to them as authenticators—certified our achievements of milestones! Our youngest sibling continues his learning to this day, and he is probably the most prolific reader among us.

* * *

"Be proud of what you do," Mama used to tell us. "Be proud of what you accomplish in whatever you decide to do." What she meant was that we were expected to be proud of whatever we attempted. It was her way of saying that if we weren't going to be proud of something we tried, we shouldn't even be attempting it. Nevertheless, her expectations created a host of challenges. That's where earning college degrees came in. Now at seventy-eight years of age, I'm thankful our parents goaded us into seeking personal achievements. Otherwise, our reaching those milestones may never have occurred. Thank you, Mama and Papa!

Mama is still foremost in my mind; she is the one in whom I laid my trust and life when I was a child. She survived the big war and ensured all four of her babies did too. But she should have died in much more splendorous surroundings. Instead she just went away forever by herself, all alone, in an old, cold house at the Corners Farm in northern Indiana. She had endured too much to just die in so common an environment. A special, bejeweled, well-lit room in heaven would have been more appropriate.

Papa told me that he did his best to kill as many WWII Japanese soldiers as he could. Meanwhile, he organized the 107th Mindanao Guerrilla Division. All this was to save his adopted country, the Philippines, for better times. Papa also survived amid great odds. He was highly successful in meeting all his objectives. But I continue to think he should have been swamped with accolades while he was alive. Papa will always be my personal hero.

My Little Sis

Becky denied that she was dying, and close to the very end (within a matter of days, anyhow) she told me that an oncologist had mentioned to her she could perhaps prolong her life a bit beyond the four years he had initially predicted, by receiving radiation treatment for her breast cancer. Her doctor had mentioned that she would still remain a terminal patient but could live longer, perhaps four weeks more. She was aghast at his diagnosis: "Why should I fight the schedule that God has set up?"

During one of our last telephone conversations, she repeated to me that she had adamantly told him, "The only radiation I'll ever receive will come from the sun, the source of life—as all believers of Eastern medicine know!" (Well, I am a believer of so-called Western medicine, and I also know that fact.)

She then continued relating to me her usual tirade about the positive aspects of Eastern medicine, including its ancient beginnings over seven thousand years ago—all which I digested without arguing that if Eastern medicine is so good, why hasn't the whole world embraced and adopted it instead of adopting Western medicine? Even then I already knew that the days of my little sis were numbered and that to initiate an argument at such a stage in her life would be pointless. Up to the very end, she had denied she was sick. Still, she had to have known her time was running out. After all, her doctor had declared her cancer to be terminal a matter of years before. When she passed on, her calendar indicated four years and three months had gone by since his initial prediction of four years. I'd say he was very good at medical estimations!

Louise and I had an opportunity to visit Becky for a few days before we departed on a trip to Scotland. Becky knew we were going, and she blessed us for traveling on English soil. "I wish I were going with you," she had said matter-of-factly, "but I'm going to have to get well first before I'm able to enjoy such a trip." We knew she would never get well again, and she probably did also. Becky passed away about 1800 on Thursday, August 6, 2007, at her home in Sacramento, California.

I will always remember exactly when Becky died. Our traveling group was touring the northernmost tip of Scotland at the time. Our motor coach came to a stop, waiting with a few automobiles for a vehicle ferry to begin loading. After waiting for a couple of hours, the driver finally made an announcement: "Well, gents and ladies, we're just not going to load today! Gale force winds are expected to continue through the night. This is a first; the ferry crossing hasn't been cancelled in the last ten years! Instead we'll just stop by the pub just ahead!"

It seems strange to admit, but after the disappointing announcement concerning the extreme weather, and observing the increasingly large waves blowing in against the shore, Louise and I turned to each other and nodded a silent understanding. The forces of nature were confirming for us that our Becky was gone at the age of sixty-eight years. She had a long, long journey from surviving as a toddler hiding out on Catalunan Pequeño in the Philippines to raising an exceptional son, Daniel, and owning her own home in Sacramento, California, USA.

*   *   *

"Among so many thorns, a flower is much welcomed." Papa used to say this of Becky, who was a rose among his brood, hinting for all within earshot that her three siblings were all boys. His opinions weren't lost on us either, because she was indeed a favorite of his.

Retrospection

From retrospection of the past seventy-eight years, I conclude there's surely a lot of living out there for just one lifetime. It's all been enjoyable, and I wouldn't change one tiny bit of my past. Even now I'm on an extended, exciting roller-coaster ride. Over the many years that have passed, I can even lay claim to developing an ability to be cool on discovering extreme and challenging surprises around corners.

*   *   *

I have learned that a lifetime can be divided into universal phases of about twenty years each:

1. Education   01–20 years
2. Application   20–40 years
3. Accumulation   40–60 years
4. Vacation   60–80 years, if all goes well
5. Dissipation   Varies

*   *   *

Often I gaze from our window on the thirty-ninth floor just to watch the city come alive. And while I am grateful to God that I have fully experienced a bountiful life up to now, I nevertheless selfishly ponder, *There just has to be* more …

While I am very grateful that "my cup runneth over," nevertheless, I conclude as I gaze over city buildings below, *There just has to be a bigger cup out there somewhere …*

*   *   *

In closing, I have had a chance to study all of them for a while. I've made up my mind. Here's how we're going to do it: we'll first fold up Jock and put him in the daypack, because he'll want to go. *C'mon, Susie Q and Buddy. Jock's folded and in the pack, and so is the water bottle. Louise is coming, along with Bonnie and Clyde. We have a long hike ahead of us. Bless my mama and my papa …*

Epilogue

My husband Jim frequently explains that he worked on writing his memoir for four and a half or five years. Recently, however, I came upon some papers in a notebook in which I found an outline / table of contents titled "Memories of War, 1941–1945." The carefully numbered list (in his typical tech-writer style and beautiful penmanship of years gone by) was exactly what he has written about in chapter 2 of this book. Then I was surprised to see the noted date was November 20, 2005—indicating that the conscious effort of working on his memoir had been going on for a period of at least ten years.

Initially I was involved only indirectly with the memoir-writing effort as Jim brought up subjects from his past that he wanted to discuss or explain—frequently, and sometimes very emotionally. He usually spent several hours every day at the computer "working on his MWIB project" (as he always refers to the title, *My Wars and In Between*), often going on into the early morning hours. During 2012, however, I realized he was losing the general ability to concentrate or focus on daily activities. His efforts at the computer were diminishing and certainly not productive. Two years of attempting to understand his condition with ongoing medical evaluation, treatments, and diagnoses followed.

Early in 2014, Jim admitted to experiencing mobility problems, besides the cognitive difficulties, and he gave up his favorite exercise of jogging while kicking and controlling a soccer ball. Finally, in 2015, he was diagnosed with diffuse Lewy body disease, and he now takes prescription medications developed for Parkinson's Disease and Alzheimer's, which are having some positive effects.

An obsession with getting his memoir submitted for publication and the frustration of not getting it done was also having a negative effect on

Jim's declining health. I discretely began getting into the writing files on his computer to see how much of his book was already written that I might be able to pull together—before offering to take on the job for him. What I found was that the storytelling part of his effort was complete, but in his recent confusion, it was all mixed up, with a great deal of duplication, residing in numerous different computer files. I was pretty sure that I could follow his outlines and eventually get it all into one document for the publisher. The remaining challenge was to convince him that the project could safely be turned over to me.

As Jim began to accept the medical condition of LBD now dominating his very existence, he also accepted my assistance on the book (and in a lot of other areas as well!)—with gratitude and appreciation, I must add. We became a team, and I am honored to take his earlier writing and presentation intent, and combine it with my organizing and computer formatting as required for publication. Above all, the work remains Jim's memoir.

Louise K. Oliver

Appendix A

A Lifetime Timeline

This lifetime timeline is a concept my wife suggested. After it was implemented, we also found it useful in finalizing the manuscript of the book. Many entries in the timeline record events, individuals, and details that are not necessarily included in the main body of the memoir but may be of chronological interest to some readers.

Year Age	Notes
1937 00	I was born Wednesday, June 30, 1937, and named James Stanley Oliver in Davao City, Mindanao, Philippines.
1938 01	My brother Bob was two years older; we lived with our parents in the family home in Davao City.
1939 02	My sister Becky was born.
1940 03	Marciana was our nanny.
1941 04	My brother Winston was born, early in WWII. Pearl Harbor was bombed, and the Japanese occupation of Davao City followed.
1942 05	We were forced out of our family home by Japanese troops and moved to one next door. Military occupation and starvation forced us from Davao City. We escaped out of the city on foot, to the farm.

1943 06   WWII continued. Mama and her three young children were living a subsistence existence on the farm.

1944 07   Still on the farm, we were hiding from the Japanese military.

1945 08   We escaped from the farm to a remote nipa hut hideout, and we then made another nighttime escape back to the farm.

1946 09   After the War, we were rescued by Papa and moved back to our home in Davao City—two blocks from our prewar home.

1947 10   I attended Palma Gil Elementary School in Davao City.

1948 11   I attended Palma Gil Elementary School in Davao City.

1949 12   Papa, Bob, Jim, and Becky moved from Davao City, Mindanao, Philippines, to the United States. We rode across the country on a bus to Akron, Indiana. I attended seventh grade in Akron, Indiana, public schools.

1950 13   We kids lived with the family of Uncle Kenneth. I attended eighth grade in Akron.

1951 14   Mama and Winston joined us from the Philippines. We all lived together now, in the Oliver family Corners Farm. I achieved the BSA First-Class rank and attended ninth grade at Akron High School.

1952 15   The family continued living at Corners Farm. I attended tenth grade at Akron High School.

1953 16   The family continued living at Corners Farm. I attended eleventh grade at Akron High School.

1954 17   The family continued living at Corners Farm. In summer I was on the staff of Camp Buffalo, the Boy Scout camp near Monticello, Indiana, and was selected into the Boy Scout honor-camper brotherhood, Order of the Arrow. I attended twelfth grade at Akron High School.

1955 18   The family continued living at Corners Farm. I earned the BSA Eagle Scout award. I was on the summer staff at Camp Buffalo. I graduated from Akron High School, where I was president of my class. I enrolled for my freshman year at Purdue University, in West Lafayette, Indiana; there I entered the AFROTC program.

1956 19   I completed my freshman year at Purdue University. During the summer, I worked on the Erie Railroad. I then began my sophomore year at Purdue.

1957 20   I completed my sophomore year at Purdue. In the summer, I was a staff member at Rocky Mountain YMCA Camp, near Estes Park, Colorado. I climbed Mt. Ypsilon (elevation 13,514 feet). In September, I began my junior year at Purdue.

1958 21   I completed my junior year at Purdue and attended the USAF Officer Summer Camp at Selfridge AFB, Michigan. In the fall, I returned to Purdue University.

1959 22   I married wife number one. I still needed more classes, so my Purdue graduation was delayed. In the fall, I was appointed AFROTC division commander (overseeing 2,200 AFROTC cadets). I also received the Military Order of the World Wars Medal while in AFROTC at Purdue. My first child, Laura Ann, was born.

1960 23   In January, I graduated from Purdue University with a bachelor of science degree in international relations and a USAF military commission. I worked at US Steel. In June, I entered into US Air Force active duty as a second lieutenant and reported for primary flight training at Graham Air Base.

1961 24   I reported for basic flying training at Reese AFB, in Texas. There I failed out. My second child, Karin Lee, was born. In late fall, I transferred to the USAF newly acquired ICBM Program to be a missiles procedures instructor at Vandenberg AFB in California.

1962 25   My instructor duties continued at Vandenberg AFB. My third child, James Reece, was born.

1963 26   My instructor duties continued at Vandenberg AFB.

1964 27   My instructor duties continued at Vandenberg AFB. I attended Squadron Officer School at Maxwell AFB Air University, in Montgomery, Alabama, for three months. Wife number one and I divorced.

1965 28   My instructor duties continued at Vandenberg AFB.

1966 29   My instructor duties continued at Vandenberg AFB. Papa died at home in Akron, Indiana; he was seventy-six years old.

1967 30   I was assigned to the Forty-Fourth SMW missile combat crew operations at Ellsworth AFB, near Rapid City, South Dakota. In the fall, I completed graduate courses in economics though the Air Force Institute of Technology extension, SDSU.

1968 31   My missile combat crew duties continued at Ellsworth AFB. I went solo backpacking at Pactola Reservoir in South Dakota.

1969 32   My missile combat crew duties continued at Ellsworth AFB. I married wife number two.

1970 33   My missile combat crew duties continued at Ellsworth AFB. My fourth child, Michael Robert, was born. From September to December, I was at Fort Bragg, in North Carolina, for schooling with the US Army at John Fitzgerald Kennedy United States Army Institute for Military Assistance.

1971 34   In January, I was assigned to the Vietnam War: Bao Trai, Hau Nghia Province, Vietnam—AFSC 2111 (Unconventional Warfare / Special Operations). In December, I returned to the United States and the ICBM Program at Ellsworth AFB.

1972 35   I was officer-in-charge of the Field Maintenance Branch at Malmstrom AFB, near Great Falls, Montana. I went solo backpacking in the Bob Marshall Wilderness Area, in Montana.

1973 36   I was officer-in-charge of the Vehicle Equipment Branch at Malmstrom AFB. I took a canoe trip near the Missouri Breaks on the Missouri River, from Great Falls, with the Colclaziers.

1974 37   My OIC duties continued at Malmstrom AFB. I was awarded the Bronze Star Medal for work in the Phoenix Program during my tour in the Vietnam War. I went solo backpacking in the Sawtooth Wilderness, Idaho. Wife number two and I divorced.

1975 38   My OIC duties continued at Malmstrom AFB. I went group backpacking in Glacier National Park, in Montana and Canada.

1976 39   My OIC duties continued at Malmstrom AFB. In June, I was assigned to Headquarters, Strategic Air Command (SAC) at the Office of the Inspector General as an ICBM maintenance inspector, Offutt AFB, in Omaha, Nebraska.

1977 40   My SAC IG duties continued at Offutt AFB. In the spring after duty days, I attended Creighton University in Omaha, taking graduate courses in International Relations. Solo backpacking: High Uinta Mountain Range, Utah.

1978 41   My SAC IG duties continued at Offutt AFB. In June, I returned to the ICBM program as maintenance supervisor of the Forty-Fourth Organizational Missile Maintenance Squadron at Ellsworth AFB, in South Dakota. I went solo backpacking in Kings Canyon National Park, California.

1979 42   I was a maintenance control officer with the Forty-Fourth Strategic Missile Wing at Ellsworth AFB.

1980 43   I was assistant to maintenance officer with the 3901 Strategic Missile Evaluation Squadron, a part of the SAC Headquarters Operations assigned to California at Vandenberg AFB. I went solo backpacking at Humbug Spires National Wilderness, in Montana.

1981 44   My SMES duties continued at Vandenberg AFB. In June, I earned a master's degree in public administration from Golden Gate University, in California. In the fall, I was reassigned as squadron commander of the 90 Organizational Missile Maintenance Squadron, strategic missile maintenance, at FE Warren AFB, in Cheyenne, Wyoming.

1982 45   My squadron commander 90 OMMS duties continued at FE Warren AFB.

1983 46   My squadron commander 90 OMMS duties continued at FE Warren AFB. I traveled to Germany solo and drove through the country.

1984 47   In January, I retired from my twenty-four-year US Air Force career. In February, I started at Martin Marietta Corporation, Denver, Colorado, as a logistics representative (LG-45).

1985 48   I continued as a logistics representative with Martin Marietta. I purchased a townhome in Aurora, Colorado. I went solo backpacking in Maroon Bells Wilderness Area, in Aspen, Colorado.

1986 49   I continued as Logistics Representative, Martin Marietta. Mama died, living alone at Corners Farm home in Akron, Indiana. She was 86 years old. I begin travelling with Louise: Vancouver, Canada; Domestic Travel: San Francisco, California.

1987 50   I continued as a logistics representative with Martin Marietta. Domestic Travel: Newport Beach/Pasadena, CA. I receive a *Technical Achievement Award* from Martin Marietta Corporation, also recognized this year as an *Outstanding IRAD Principle Investigator*. Solo backpacking: San Juan Mountains, Durango, Colorado; camping with brother Winston: Eagles Nest Wilderness—Vail, Colorado.

1988 51　I continued as a logistics representative with Martin Marietta. I traveled to Santa Barbara, Lompoc, Santa Maria, and Vandenberg AFB in California. I visited family in Great Falls, Montana. Louise and I traveled to Brisbane, Australia, for the World Expo.

1989 52　I continued as a logistics representative with Martin Marietta. Louise and I went white-water canoeing and camping on the Gunnison River, in Colorado. I went solo backpacking in the Mount of the Holy Cross Wilderness Area, in Minturn, Colorado.

1990 53　I continued as a logistics representative with Martin Marietta. Louise and I went white-water canoeing and camping on the Green River, in Utah. We also visited Kyoto, Japan, for the International Expo.

1991 54　In April, I was laid off from Martin Marietta Corporation, Strategic Systems Division, Denver, Colorado. I began my second retirement. I married wife number three, Louise Kuhn. We honeymooned at the Grand Canyon, in Arizona. We went white-water canoeing and camping on the North Platte River, in Wyoming. We also went to Sacramento, California, to visit family.

1992 55　I had a six-month assignment as an independent contractor for Martin Marietta Corporation, working on an FAA technical proposal in Washington, DC. Louise and I established our small business, Questers Advisory Group, Inc., in Aurora, Colorado. We visited family in Ft. Wayne, Indiana. We also traveled to Seville, Spain, for the World Expo.

1993 56　I was retired; my part-time writing career continued. Louise and I traveled to Calaveras County, California, for family visits and touring. We also traveled to Wichita, Kansas, for a family visit. I went solo backpacking in the Hunter-Fryingpan Wilderness Area (Independence Pass), near Aspen, Colorado.

1994 57 My part-time writing career continued. Louise and I began publishing a monthly retirement home newsletter as Questers Communications (which continued for six more years). We traveled to Wichita, Kansas, for a family visit.

1995 58 My part-time writing career continued. I sold my townhome, and Louise and I purchased a condominium in a downtown Denver high-rise building.

1996 59 My part-time writing career continued. Louise and I traveled to Anchorage, Alaska, for the starting events of the annual Iditarod Trail Sled Dog Race, and to Wichita, Kansas, and to Silver Lake, Indiana, for family visits.

1997 60 My part-time writing career continued. We published our first book—*Grandpa's Very Short Stories*. Louise and I traveled to Hong Kong and China; made family visits to Wichita and Fall River, Kansas. I went solo backpacking in the Hunter-Fryingpan Wilderness Area (Independence Pass), near Aspen, Colorado.

1998 61 Louise and I traveled to Fredonia and Wichita, Kansas, for family visits; went to North Platte, Nebraska, to see the Sand Hill Crane migration; visited Lisbon, Portugal, for the World Expo; took a cruise to Alaska's Inside Passage; toured on the Amazon River, and visited Machu Picchu in Peru.

1999 62 Louise and I traveled to South Dakota to see Mt. Rushmore, Bear Butte, and Badlands National Park; went to Yellowstone National Park, in Montana and Wyoming; visited family in Wichita, Kansas; and took a cruise to the Panama Canal.

2000 63 Louise and I visited Egypt; Delft, the Netherlands; the Danube River; Hanover, Germany (for the World Expo); went to Akron, Indiana, for my high school class reunion; went white-water canoeing and camping on the Gunnison River, in Colorado. We also traveled to the Antarctic Peninsula (our seventh continent!).

2001 64   Louise and I went to Ft. Bragg to revisit some of my Vietnam War memories. We also went to Wilmington, North Carolina, for a family visit, and took a cruise of the Rivieras and Capitals of Europe.

2002 65   Louise and I visited North Platte, Nebraska, to see the Sand Hill Crane migration and traveled to Poros, Greece.

2003 66   Louise and I went to Wilmington, North Carolina, and Park City, Kansas, for family visits. We visited Akron, Indiana, for my high school reunion. We also traveled the Columbia River from Portland, Oregon, following the travels of Lewis and Clark on a riverboat.

2004 67   Louise and I visited Mexico's Copper Canyon. We went to Lafayette, Indiana, and Purdue University for an Oliver family visit. We also traveled to Wichita, Kansas, for a family visit. We took a cruise and land tour of Alaska's Inside Passage, Prudhoe Bay, and Denali National Park.

2005 68   Louise and I traveled to Finland and the fjords of Norway. We visited Wichita and Park City, Kansas, for family visits. We also took a fifty-one-day cruise to Mexico, South America, and the South Pacific.

2006 69   Louise and I continued our long cruise visiting New Zealand, Tasmania, and ending in Sydney, Australia. We went to Sacramento and Merced, California, and Plato, Missouri, for family visits, and we visited my son Jim, training for Iraq in El Paso, Texas. We also took a tour and small ship cruise of wild and ancient Britain.

2007 70   Louise and I traveled from Moscow to St. Petersburg, Russia, on a Russian Waterways riverboat trip. We hosted an Oliver and Jackson (Louise) family retreat in Estes Park, Colorado, celebrating our seventieth birthday year—at the YMCA camp of the Rockies. We also took a grand tour of Scotland. Little sis—Fé Rebecca Oliver (Becky)—died of breast cancer at home in Sacramento, California.

2008 71   Louise and I took another fifty-two-day cruise from Sydney, Australia, to Istanbul, Turkey. We went to Wichita, Kansas, for a family visit. We traveled to the lakes of Northern Italy and the Swiss Alps.

2009 72   Louise and I traveled Eastern Europe (Romania, Bulgaria, Croatia, and Hungary) via a riverboat trip on the Danube River from the Black Sea. Louise and I were both diagnosed with cancer in December.

2010 73   In January, Louise had surgery to remove breast cancer. In March, I underwent cryotherapy to treat prostate cancer. Louise and I visited Croatia, Greece, Egypt, Israel, and Turkey on an ancient mysteries cruise.

2011 74   Louise and I took a riverboat trip on the Rhine and Moselle Rivers. In November, I began seriously writing my second book (this memoir). In December, we hosted the Ollie Bear Cousins Reunion in downtown Denver.

2012 75   Louise and I traveled to Johannesburg, South Africa; Victoria Falls; Zimbabwe; and Botswana and went on a river safari. We went to Vail, Colorado, for a Jackson family retreat in western Colorado. We also took a cruise to Canada and the East Coast of the United States.

2013 76   Louise and I toured Patagonia and took a small ship cruise of Chile (Torres del Pane National Park) and Argentina (ice fields and glaciers). We went to Avon, Colorado, for the annual Jackson family retreat. We also took a thirty-five-day large ship cruise titled "Voyage of the Vikings," which took us to Canada, Iceland, Greenland, Norway, and the Netherlands.

2014 77   Louise and I visited Avon, Colorado, for the annual Jackson family retreat and went to South Haven, Michigan, for an extended stay at our new cottage near Lake Michigan.

2015 78   I am diagnosed with Diffuse Lewy Body Disease, which effects mobility, cognitive, and behavioral aspects of life. Louise and I spend most of the summer at our cottage in Michigan. We return home to Denver and begin adjusting to a new lifestyle. Louise and I work on completing this memoir.

2016 79   My memoir is finally published. Louise and I continue to enjoy living in our high-rise condo in downtown Denver, Colorado.

A Biographic Summary

Lt. Col. James S. Oliver, USAF (Ret.)

My birth certificate shows that I was born on June 30, 1937, to Flora and Augustus Oliver in Cota Bato on the island of Mindanao, Philippine Islands. All original records were destroyed during WWII, and therefore my official birthplace since then has been Davao City, Mindanao. This is indeed where our family lived for the first few years of my life. Mama was born in Iloilo, Philippines, and Papa was from Akron, Indiana, in the United States. Also, since the Philippines belonged to the United States at that time, I have always been a US citizen.

Transitions

When I was a child of about five, a Japanese warplane dive-bombed the administrative buildings of Davao City, Mindanao, Philippines. The event marked the beginning of almost five years of World War II. When the war was over, our family found that records had been destroyed, and virtually all buildings and the school system were in a shambles. That's why Mama and Papa decided to try our luck in Akron, Indiana—my papa's home grounds. The year was 1949. Mama and Winston had stayed in Davao City to administer the farm and both city homes. About a year later, they both came to Akron to join the rest of the Oliver family.

When we (Papa; my elder brother, Bob; me; and my younger sister, Fe Rebecca [Becky]) arrived in Akron, Indiana, I experienced some expressions of cultural differences, especially from teachers—to whom we all look for guidance, and who should have known better! Right off the bat, I was impressed by the generosity of the little town's residents, as well as that of my close relatives. I never once experienced any tendency from my classmates to bully me because of racial differences, although I had anticipated my classmates would be the most likely source of bullying. In fact, it was the teachers—the grown-ups from whom we expected answers—who were the sources of racial bullying. Quite naturally, I liked my classmates while at the same time I disdained certain teachers.

Academically, I was subjected to a few tests in a closed room by officials of the Akron school system. I then was enrolled in the seventh grade, at the same level as other kids my age. That's the point at which I began my integration into a new culture. I liked my personal popularity; I was lucky to be voted into a class office every year since my enrollment. This trend continued to my graduation in 1955, the year I was voted president of my graduating class.

Postgraduation

After graduating from high school in 1955, I joined a crew maintaining Erie Railroad tracks westward to Rochester. My group was assigned to dig communication cable trenches, lay steel rails, and paint creosote onto oak ties. I found it to be backbreaking work. For an entire summer, I never felt a cool day between June and September. In fact, one day in July 1955, while working next to the heat of the railroad bed of white rocks just east of Akron, I experienced a recurrence of malaria chills. (Several years later, while in the Vietnam War, a recurrent attack of malaria happened once more. At that time, a US Air Force flight surgeon told me I would carry dormant malaria germs in me until the day I die.)

Earnings from working on Erie Railroad tracks gave me the financial ability to attend Purdue University in the fall of 1955. Tuition at Purdue was relatively inexpensive for me because I was an Indiana resident. During the winter months, my earnings came from the Cary Residence Hall dining room, where I worked clearing dishes after classes were finished for the day. One time, when I was able to schedule a Purdue visit for my mama and papa, I was able to save and present to them six paychecks—which, of course, they refused.

After two years of schooling at Purdue, engineering and mathematics courses were giving me a great deal of trouble. So I switched to the humanities and then made As and Bs in almost every course in which I was enrolled. Within four semesters of the big switch, I was appointed by the professor of air science (PAS) the cadet division commander of Purdue's 2,200 Air Force ROTC (Reserve Officer Training Corps) cadets, which included the freshman and sophomore cadets enrolled in AFROTC. By this time, I had also earned the Military Order of the World Wars award sponsored by the Chicago Tribune Newsgroup. A few months later, I had earned a bachelor's degree in international relations and a commission as a second lieutenant in the US Air Force active-duty reserves.

Career Number One

Pilot training in Florida began in June 1960 at Graham Air Base, which was largely run by civilian-contract pilots, most of whom came from the Korean War. I passed primary flight training, but a year later, at Reese AFB, in Texas, I had problems with cross-country flights, and I failed basic flight training. As a result, I didn't become a pilot, but I did earn a Regular Forces Commission and was assigned to an intercontinental ballistic missile (ICBM) unit in California and was transferred a few years later to South Dakota. *That* is roller-coasting: screeching downs followed by breathless ups!

From Strategic Air Command (SAC) missile combat crew commander duties in South Dakota, I was sent to the US Army Psychological Warfare School at Ft. Bragg, North Carolina, for training in special operations. In January 1971, I was then sent to the Vietnam War to join a mixed civilian-and-military team on the Phoenix program. After a year with MACV (Military Assistance Command–Vietnam) Advisory Team 43, I was back in ICBMs as a maintenance officer in Montana. I then joined the SAC inspector general team at Offutt AFB, in Nebraska, which is also headquarters for the Strategic Air Command. Five base assignments later, in 1984, I retired at F. E. Warren AFB, in Wyoming, as an ICBM maintenance squadron commander—after a twenty-four-year career in the

USAF. I moved into a townhouse in Denver, Colorado, because I didn't want to mow grass or shovel snow.

Family Then

I married in my junior year at Purdue University. We were divorced five years later, sharing three children: Laura, now in Colorado; Karin, with a master's degree and her family in North Carolina; and corporate pilot (and former US Army Black Hawk helicopter and straight-wing instructor pilot) James, in Louisiana. I vowed never to marry again, but after five years, I met a teacher in Rapid City, South Dakota, who had the mannerisms of a Hollywood movie star, and I married again. After five more years and a son Mike, we divorced during readjustments on my return from my yearlong assignment in special operations and unconventional warfare during the Vietnam War.

Career Number Two

After retirement from the USAF in 1984, I hired into Martin Marietta Aerospace Corporation as a logistics engineer and then was laid off in 1991. On my departure, I opted for early retirement at fifty-five years of age.

Family Now

I met Louise in 1986. She had just transitioned to Denver from her management career in the Colorado ski industry. We dated for five years, and by the end of that period, nothing terrible had happened. So I set aside eighteen bachelor years and a five-year fear, and I remarried in 1991. In the early years, we often sponsored family Sunday brunches, mostly for older relatives. International travel became a regular activity, even before we were totally retired. White-water canoe trips were a great pleasure for several years. Now we look forward to spending more of the summer months at our cottage near the shores of Lake Michigan. We are very happy, and I've often wondered where this fascinating woman has been all my life!

Career Number Three

Louise was chief executive officer and I was president of our home-based company, Questers Advisory Group, Inc., which we formed in 1992. Now our contracting business is inactive, but for several years, we focused on business analysis as well as literary and commercial writing. Her last consulting contract resulted in a permanent job in downtown Denver, from which Louise retired in 1997. We also had a contract to edit teaching guides for the Head Start regional office in Phoenix, Arizona. In addition, for several years we wrote, edited, and published monthly retirement-community newsletters for 3,200 readers. In 1997, we wrote and published our first book, *Grandpa's Very Short Stories*, a collection of thirty-six very short stories (ISBN 1-57502-635-X). (We have forty more very short stories just dying to be published.)

Travels

We were avid worldwide travelers, as detailed in chapter 7 of this memoir. In 2013, we wound up our lifelong travels with a thirty-five-day cruise aboard the MS *Veendam* of Holland America Lines, from Boston, Massachusetts, past Greenland and Iceland, on to Norway, and back. Long ago, we had decided this was how we were going to do it—travel as much as possible in the early years of retirement and finish it up before we got too old to drag our bags easily.

Sports

We both were skiers (downhill and cross-country), snowshoers, mountain bikers, and canoeists with Denver Museum groups. During my military career, I won five USAF base racquetball championships. I also had a passion for solo backpacking, which is described in greater detail in chapter 7. I still weigh 155 high-school pounds, but I no longer move around as easily as I did in those days.

Hobbies

In earlier years, I collected postal-stamp sheets, kachina dolls, and Plains Indian pewter statuettes. In our downtown condominium, I have picked up a fascination for nurturing a large collection of houseplants (of the corn plant, philodendron, pothos, and spider plant varieties). They thrive with a little watering and extensive personal attention. Also, they really like the unimpeded morning sunlight near the balcony doors up high in our downtown condominium.

Glossary

Abbreviations, Acronyms, Definitions, Pronunciations

Pronunciations of Spanish, Filipino, and American English words are based upon International Phonetics Association phonics use and practice. If more-correct pronunciations are desired, readers should please seek an expert in the field.

Pronunciation of each syllable of a word occurs, wherein a dot (.) represents a short pause; a dash (-), a longer (but almost imperceptibly longer) pause or delay. The letters of a syllable are capitalized to show where emphasis should be placed in the word. (Lowercase letters carry no emphasis at all.)

AA: Antiaircraft.

abaca: A strong fiber from the leafstalk of a banana, native to the Philippines; also known as Manila hemp.

Apo (AH-poh): Mount Apo, a volcano on Mindanao, Philippines.

AFIT: Air Force Institute of Technology.

AFROTC: Air Force Reserve Officer Training Corps.

AFSC: Air Force specialty code.

bakyá (BOCK-yah): A sturdy wooden shoe.

Bao Trai (BOW, as in bow-wow; and TRY, as in try again …): Team headquarters, Vietnam.

Bwisit (*BWEE.sit*): Visayan for "one who plays with his food."

camotes (Kah.MOW-tas): A type of wild yam root crop.

carabao (Kahrah—BOW): A domesticated water buffalo.

Catalunan: Relates to the region in northeast Spain termed Catalonia; Barcelona is the main city.

Catalunan Grande: Rural plantation areas outside of Davao City, Mindanao.

Catalunan Pequeño (kah.tah-LOO.nahn peh-KEN.yoh): A rural area, also called Sunny Brook Farm.

CCTS: Combat Crew Training Squadron.

Colclazier (Kol.CLAY-zee.*yurr*): Family name of good friends at Malmstrom AFB.

cold turkey: Abrupt, complete cessation of use, without a period of gradual adjustment.

cogon: A type of tall grass, especially in southeastern Asia, used for thatching and fodder.

datu (DAH.too): King or chief, as in Datu Lapu-Lapu, who is possibly related to Flora Oliver.

Davao (DAH-vow) City: A major city in Mindanao, Philippines.

EWO: Emergency war order.

FMB: Field maintenance branch.

gwayabanos (gwyah.BAHN-noss): A wild jungle fruit with a leathery skin.

hamadryad: Cobra.

High Uintas (high yoo.WIN-tahs): A mountain range in Utah.

ICBM: Intercontinental ballistic missile.

IRAD: Independent research and development.

Jacinto (hah.SIN-toh): A street in downtown Davao City, Mindanao, Philippines.

JFKUSAIMA: John Fitzgerald Kennedy United States Army Institute for Military Assistance.

JUSPAO: Joint United States Public Affairs Office.

Kawá-Kawá (COW.wah-COW.wah): A remote jungle village on Mindanao in the 1940s.

Kempeitai (*KEM-peh.tye*): A division of the WWII Japanese military forces.

kwashiorker (kwah.shee-OR.kurr): Severe malnutrition in infants and children.

Lapu-Lapu (LAH.poo-LAH.poo): An ancient king in the Philippine Islands.

lanzones (Lahn.ZOHN-ness): A small, pulpy fruit with a bitter seed.

LCC: Launch control center.

LCF: Launch control facility.

LOH: Light observation helicopter.

LST: Landing ship, tank.

Mactan (mac-TAHN): Small island near Iloilo, Philippines.

MACV: Military Assistance Command–Vietnam.

Mapa (MAH.pah): A street in downtown Davao City, Mindanao, Philippines.

MCCC: Missile combat crew commander.

MCO: Maintenance control officer.

memoir: A written account in which someone describes his or her past experiences.

mestizo (mess.TEE-zoe, the last syllable as in "toe"): An individual of mixed race.

MiMS: Minuteman Maintenance Squadron.

Mindanao (MINH-dah.now): Largest island of the Philippine Archipelago.

Mintal (minh.TAHL): A small town that connects with Talomo near Davao City.

Muncie (MUN.see): A city in central Indiana; home city of Ball State University.

narra (NAH.rah): An exceptionally hard wood from the Philippines.

nipa hut: A small bamboo shelter made of native materials, with a grass-thatched roof.

NVA: North Vietnamese Army.

OIC: Officer-in-charge.

OMB: Organizational Maintenance Branch.

OMMS: Organizational Missile Maintenance Squadron.

ouzel (OO.zell): a small waterbird.

papayas (pah.PIE-yas): a wild native tree fruit.

PCS: Permanent change of station.

plantains: Green banana-shaped fruit that can be boiled to prepare for eating.

pomelo (pronounced PUH.meh.low): Fruit similar to a grapefruit, generally a greenish color.

PPA: Province psychological advisor.

PTSD: Post-traumatic stress disorder.

ROTC: Reserve Officer Training Corps.

SAC: Strategic Air Command.

SDSU: South Dakota State University.

shrapnel: Small metal pieces that scatter outward from an exploding bomb, shell, or mine.

SMES: Strategic Missile Evaluation Squadron.

SMW: Strategic Missile Wing.

SOSA: Special operations staff advisor.

SST: Sort, select, talk (first aid for PTSD).

Tagalog (tuh.GAH-logg): Native language of the Philippines.

Talomo (tah.LOH-moh; tah.LOM-uh): A beach area near Davao City.

TDY: Temporary duty away from home assignment.

Tiongko (TYONG-ko): A downtown street in Davao City, Mindanao, Philippines.

USAF: United States Air Force.

USAFFE: United States Army Forces in the Far East.

USIA: United States Information Service.

USSR: Union of Soviet Socialist Republics.

VCI: Vietcong infrastructure.

VECB: Vehicle and Equipment Control Branch.

VEOC: Vehicle equipment, officer-in-charge.

VHF: Very high frequency—a type of radio.

VIP: Very important person.

VN: Vietnam.

Visayan (vee.SIGH-yan) or Visayas (vee.SY-yus): An island in the central Philippines.

wakwak (WOCK-wock): A tree near Sunny Brook Farm with mysterious/evil abilities.

WWII: World War II.

Printed in the United States
By Bookmasters